# Mehal Mał

# UNLOCKING PSYCHIC POTENTIAL

### Shining a light on who you truly are

# **Copyright:**

Copyright 2021 – Mehal Mahipal

First Edition

All rights reserved. No part of the book may be reproduced in any manner without written permission from the author or publisher.

Cover and book design by: Ema Townsend

Editor: Rachel Hutchins

The intention of this book is to educate, inspire and to use pictures as well as quotes to illustrate themes arising from the author's analysis and synthesis of a wide range of personal experiences in the spiritual field. Any of the pictures used in this book are fully acknowledged with copyrights by their owners or available to the public. Such pictures used for illustrative purposes are intended to come under the "Fair use of copyright" restrictions. All pictures from every source are fully acknowledged and referenced.

If you would like to get permission to use any of the copyright protected information published in this book for your business, or any other commercial use (for your products, to teach to your students or any use for business) you can request our copyright license agreement by emailing to info@mehalmahipal.com

ISBN: 9798701064193

# GET YOUR

# FREE Meditation Bundle

2 x Meditation Sessions
& Sacred Ritual

For direct download
Visit:

# www.unlockingpsychicpotential.com

# Enrol now!

# SELF STUDY COURSE

12 Video/Audio Lectures & Printable transcripts
Proven methods & interactive assessments

**Bonus:** over **180 minutes** of Audio Meditations

*"Shine a light on who you truly are"*

### Learn at your own pace
### With

www.unlockingpsychicpotential.com

This book is dedicated to my friend

**<u>Tyler</u>**

1985 – 2014

"What is a friend?

A single soul dwelling in two bodies."

- Aristotle -

## About Mehal Mahipal

Mehal Mahipal is a Spiritual Teacher, Astrology Tarot Card Reader and Astroshamanic Healer. For over a decade, she has studied with mentors and teachers around the world, following her own spiritual journey and expanding her skills. Many hours of self-discovery, meditation, learning and collaboration have led her to the creation of this book.

The time has come for her to pass on her knowledge about Spiritual growth and Psychic Development with the intention that more people will be able to discover their true potential.

Mehal Mahipal offers 1-2-1 Readings, Teaching Sessions as well as Self-Study Courses and Meditation Recordings to assist you on your personal journey.

For more information visit **www.mehalmahipal.com** or **www.unlockingpsychicpotential.com**

Born and raised in Germany, she finally moved to the United Kingdom in 2014 after many years of travelling around the world.

# Contents

| | |
|---|---|
| Dedication | vii |
| About the Author | ix |
| 0.01 How I know that you have Psychic Potential | 1 |
| 0.02 My Story | 4 |
| Introduction - A Simple Structure to Psychic Development | 10 |
|     I   Self Assessment | 13 |
|     II  Foundation | 14 |
|     III Advancement | 15 |
| Part I - Self Assessment Test | 17 |
|     1.1 Results of Test: Empath | 21 |
|         Exercise | 22 |
|         Signs we have taken on too much | 23 |
|         The Menstrual Cycle | 24 |
|         Self Help | 25 |
|         Exercises | 28 |
|     1.2 Results of Test: Intuitive | 29 |
|         Next Steps | 31 |
|     1.3 Results of Test: Awakened Intuitive | 32 |
|         Next Steps | 35 |
|     Why Develop your Psychic Abilities? | 36 |
| Part II - What are Psychic Abilities and Why do we have them? | 38 |
|     2.1 Psychic Powers | 42 |
|     2.2 The Clair Senses | 44 |
|         **Clairvoyance** | 45 |
|         Psychic Vision and Mediumship | 46 |
|         Eileen Garrett and the British Airship | 48 |
|         Visions and Prophesies | 49 |
|         Apparitions | 51 |
|         My Real Life Story | 57 |
|         Telepathy and Mind Reading | 59 |
|         Zenner card Experiments | 61 |
|         Remote Viewing | 64 |
|         Exercise 1 – Training your Clairvoyance | 66 |
|         Ghosts and Spirits | 68 |
|         The Fox Sisters and The Hydesville Rappings | 70 |
|         Frederic W.H. Myers | 73 |
|         Mediumship, the Law and Brave Pioneers | 74 |
|         Witch Hunts and Trials | 75 |
|         Knowing your Own Story | 76 |
|         Traditional Methods of Spirit Communication: | 81 |
|             Table Tipping | 81 |

| | |
|---|---|
| Ouija Board | 82 |
| Spiritualist Seances | 84 |
| Physical Mediumship | 85 |
| Spirit Cabinet Seances | 87 |
| Using the Spirit Cabinet | 88 |
| Pendulum | 95 |
| Ancient Spirit Communication | 96 |
| Other Ancient Spirit Communications | 100 |
| Ancient Rome and Mysticism | 100 |
| Greece | 102 |
| Spiritual Principles | 103 |
| **Clairaudience** | 106 |
| Shamans | 107 |
| Prophets | 107 |
| Channellers | 108 |
| Artists | 109 |
| Healers | 109 |
| Crisis | 110 |
| Recovery | 110 |
| Greek Sleeping Temples | 110 |
| Near Death Experience | 112 |
| Spiritualist Medium | 112 |
| Super Tip! | 113 |
| **Clairsentience** | 102 |
| Buddhism | 103 |
| Exercises | 105 |
| Meditation | 106 |
| **Clairgustance** | 114 |
| Exercise | 117 |
| **Clairtangency** | 121 |
| Psychic Detectives | 123 |
| Spiritualist Mediums | 123 |
| **Clairscent** | **123** |
| Real Life Story – Yogesh Kumar | 124 |
| Exercise | 126 |
| Part III - Advancing in your Journey | 128 |
| 3.1 How to Train Your Psychic Abilities | 128 |
| Open Circles | 129 |
| Development Classes | 130 |
| Workshops | 130 |
| Online Courses | 130 |
| Offline/Home Study Courses | 131 |
| Private 1-2-1 Tuition | 132 |

| | |
|---|---|
| Life Itself | 132 |
| 3.2 Forms of Expression | 132 |
| Exercise | 134 |
| Test Results | 135 |
| **Paranormal Investigator** | 136 |
| Harry Price | 137 |
| Ufology | 138 |
| Parapsychology | 139 |
| Demonology | 139 |
| Space Clearing | 139 |
| Cryptozoology | 140 |
| Next Steps | 141 |
| **Psychic** | 142 |
| Tarot Card Reader | 142 |
| Psychic Artist | 143 |
| Spirit Guide Painting | 144 |
| Aura Photography | 145 |
| Psychic Medium in Paranormal Investigations | 147 |
| My Real Life Story | 147 |
| Psychic Detective | 147 |
| Next Steps | 148 |
| **Spiritualist Medium** | 149 |
| Automatic Writer Medium | 150 |
| Art and Spiritualist Mediumship | 151 |
| Trance Medium | 153 |
| Further Research | 153 |
| Next Steps | 154 |
| **Healing Expression** | 156 |
| Reiki Healer | 156 |
| Spiritual Healer | 157 |
| Trance Healer | 157 |
| Further Research | 157 |
| Healing with Creative Art | 157 |
| Next Steps | 158 |
| **Shamanic Practitioner** | 160 |
| Different types of Shamanism | 160 |
| Herbalism | 161 |
| Healing the Earth | 161 |
| Other forms of Energy Medicine | 161 |
| Next Steps | 162 |
| 3.3 15 Tools to start Unlocking your Psychic Potential | 163 |
| Crystals | 163 |

| | |
|---|---|
| Tarot and Oracle Cards | 163 |
| Psychometry | 164 |
| Photo | 165 |
| Automatic Writing | 165 |
| Art | 165 |
| Colours | 165 |
| Dreams | 166 |
| Spirit Cabinet | 166 |
| People | 166 |
| TV | 167 |
| Trance State | 167 |
| Reading | 167 |
| Meditation | 167 |
| Flower Remedies | 167 |
| Stages of Development Quiz Calculations and Answers | 169 |
| Forms of Expression Quiz Calculations and Answers | 170 |
| Book List for Further Reading | 171 |
| Further Contacts and Organisations | 177 |
| Acknowledgements | 182 |
| Special Thanks | 183 |
| Resources and References | 185 |
| Illustrations | 189 |

"The students of this philosophy may well decide humanity's destiny.

In beginning your inquiry into the universal forces, which may be used for
good or for ill, you are being given a key to the future – a key that may be used to bring man out of his prison of materialism and violence and into the bright light of his highest fulfilment, or which may be used to lock, with dread finality, the door that seals him into a self-chosen doom.

The issues are delicately balanced.

The forces of materialism are noisy, they get the headlines.

Those who are influenced by sensational media therefore think the worst is inevitable. But beneath the surface of headlined events is a movement comparable to the build-up of great ground swell.

This movement is the silent power of man's inner spiritual self.

If we believe that spiritual thought-power is an actual current of energy as real as an electric current, that is the most tremendous force in the universe, it is reasonable to believe that the thought of our thousands of students would have tremendous impact on the world."

Ernest Holmes – *The Science of Mind*, 1951

# 0.01. How I know that you have psychic potential

I know you have psychic potential because you hold this book in your hand! If something inside of you has sparked an interest, is intrigued or just wants to find out more, I know what that feeling is. I felt it myself many years ago, it was never wrong and it led me to write this book.

We have a clear indicator inside of ourselves which I want to call the psychic force. This force allows us to make decisions, uncover potential and live a more meaningful and purposeful life. However, it is up to us how we are using, trusting in and directing this psychic force that moves through us.

The psychic force is different to the life force, though they come from the same origin. While the life force gives life to all living organisms, the psychic force provides the soul aspect. Many people are not aware of the psychic force inside of them and therefore totally miss out on their true potential. The psychic force can be understood as the soul's energy, consciousness that makes itself seen and heard in many different ways. The more we understand the movements of this force, the more we can use it to direct our lives in a much better way. Your intuition is the direct link to this force and will help you to clearly direct it in the right ways if you know how to do it. Psychic impressions which come through clairvoyance, clairaudience, clairsentience and others are there to help you to understand what you cannot comprehend with the logical mind in the first place. It is the power to feel what is right, to see what might come and to allow oneself to step into another reality that is not accessible for everyone.

I know that everyone holds a psychic potential and it is only when we start to explore it that we will grow into the person we were meant to be. If we are able to find the right mentors and teachers then those people will be able to help us to unlock our inner, most hidden abilities and assist us to transform into someone totally new. We will gain insights into a world that was previously hidden to us and our horizon will expand. Along this path of discovering psychic potential, we will not only find ourselves but also others. People who suddenly flow into our life, provide counsel, support and opportunities to express ourselves in totally new ways. Like-minded souls we have longed for all our life will finally come knocking on our door and we will enter a world in which we feel understood and at home.

This is what I encountered when I finally acknowledged the potential that always resided within me. I suddenly felt that I was part of something bigger, bigger than I ever dreamt of. I met more and more people who were also on the way to developing and exploring their potential and I knew that together we could do great things. I deeply felt that if even more people would understand what they were capable of achieving, if they only understood the potential that was hidden inside of them – the world would be a totally different place.

I know that you have psychic potential and I am here to help you to unlock it!

This book will provide you with over ten years of personal experience in psychic development, my accumulated studies of SPIRITUALISM, THEOSOPHY, SHAMANISM and OCCULTISM. I have brought together my understanding which I gained in watching hundreds of students develop, and in working with very well-trained teachers. Furthermore, it is inspired by my work as a translator for over seven years at the Arthur Findlay College and the mediums who I worked for all over Europe. It holds the wisdom of all the teachers who taught me seen and unseen and those I came in touch with. I have brought together insights, research, experiments and knowledge which I discussed with friends and colleagues.
Mostly, the book is based on my personal teachings and understanding of psychic phenomena and its expression. It details how I teach it to my own students.

The book is written in an easy-to-understand way so that everybody, no matter their stage of development, can understand it.
The steps are easy to follow and you will save a lot of money by allowing this book to guide you.

I want this book to help you to become the best you can be, to unlock your potential. My greatest wish is that you will gain confidence and trust in yourself.

If you learn from me, you will learn from them and I am forever grateful to anyone who contributed to this book, knowingly and unknowingly. It is my aim to fill the gap of psychic understanding, to further pass on the ways of those who once walked this earth and devoted their time and life to teach further psychic progress.

It allows you to dive deep into your personal spiritual development and there will be doors opening for you that were closed before.
At the end of the book you will find a whole list of books and literature, new and old, that allow you to study further. Many of these titles you maybe would never have come across and they are true treasure on your way to discovering your spiritual potential.

This is my gift to you.

**Mehal Mahipal**

Saltburn by the sea, November 2020

# 0.02. My Story

**"We travel, some of us forever, to seek other states, other lives, other souls."**
**- Anais Nin -**

I always felt very deeply. Nothing would pass by unnoticed or unfelt. My deep, compassionate nature was a blessing at times when I understood what other people went through. However, there were also times in which it felt like a burden or a curse. When I got caught up in the wrongdoing of the world and lost myself in hopelessness and helplessness.
There were times when I said to my mother that I didn't want to be a human because they do awful things. And I surely didn't want to be like them. Often, I found myself totally alienated from my surroundings, especially towards my birth family and the country I lived in. Germany never felt home to me and I didn't understand how it could be like home to others.

Even though my parents cared about me, I still had this innermost feeling of separation and homelessness. This even went so far that I truly believed that I was adopted, otherwise surely I should have felt connected to my family? I believed that could be the only explanation. I felt this so deeply that I started to ask myself where my "real" family was and why had they given me away?
One day when I was in one of these states again, I had very vivid pictures appearing in front of me. I saw old stone buildings, tiny roads with cobbles and street lanterns that I have never ever seen in my country. I loved those places and tried to spend more time daydreaming about them.

One day, when I was about ten years of age, I walked into the living room of our house and my mother was watching TV. I looked at the TV and saw old stone buildings, tiny roads with cobbles and these street lanterns that I had never seen before. My heart started racing, something inside of me couldn't take my eyes off the TV.
My mother looked at me, "Are you okay Julie?"
I started stuttering and said, "Mum, I know this place. Oh my God, I have been there many times before."
My mum smiled, "Well Julie, this is in England. I don't think that you have actually been there. We have never been to England before."

I knew that I was right, "No, really. I have been there before. I remember this place. I need to go back. This is where my family lived before you adopted me."

"Adopted you? What are you talking about? You are not adopted!"
I felt the anger building up inside of me. I knew no one would believe me but I also knew that I was right and I had to go there.
"I am adopted. Because I was going into a school where students live at school. There was a huge garden with massive trees and flowers. I can remember it very clearly and I need to go back. So send me back. I don't belong here."
My mum just looked at me and stayed quiet. I stormed out of the room, slammed the door and started crying my eyes out.
Why did they not let me go back home? What did I do to be abandoned like this and have to stay here? I didn't understand.

A few months later I had a very vivid dream:
'I dreamt that I was walking in the woods. In the distance I could see a castle (manor house) made of red brick stones. The building looked beautiful and radiated a sense of peace and comfort. I wondered who would be living there in such a big manor house. I was intrigued and wanted to find out because I had never seen such a building before and I was keen to find out more about it. The closer I got, the more I felt as if I actually knew the place, something inside of me just felt so familiar with it. I felt so drawn to it that I started walking faster. The faster I walked, the more the manor house seemed to move into the distance away from me and I got more and more lost in the woods. Desperately I tried to change direction, maybe there was another way to get there. The night began to fall and soon I would not be able to see anything – this scared me a little bit. Suddenly I reached a small lake, in the middle of the woods, and when I looked through the trees I could see the manor house in the distance. So, somehow, I must be on the right track. I saw the lights shining through the big windows, a sense of comfort and peace overcame me. I had to reach there before it got totally dark, otherwise I would not know what to do. After another hour of walking I totally lost my way and I couldn't see either the lake, or the house any more. I was lost and I was scared. My heart felt like breaking and I questioned again, why was I abandoned? Why did no one come to help me?

Desperate, cold and lonely I started crying. Not knowing where to go and where I was. Out of nowhere, suddenly a woman with long brown hair appeared in front of me. She wore a beautiful white cotton dress and her

feet didn't touch the earth. She was hovering off the ground somehow. "Don't cry little girl – I know the way to the castle. Just follow me!"
Hope sparked inside of me and I followed the lady in white through the woods. We went deeper and deeper into the forest and it got darker and darker. The mist in the woods seemed to get thicker with every step we took and suddenly I couldn't see the woman any more. I shouted and looked everywhere but she was nowhere to be seen. My heart cringed and I felt sudden pain in my chest, a burning, a longing for something that I had never felt before in my life. I needed to find my way to this castle, if not I would never be whole again….!'
The next moment I woke up. I felt betrayed, played at, lost and the pain in my chest was real. I could feel it, it was a burning, a stinging longing that made me want to go back into the dream. Into the other world to find this castle, to find my peace.
I tried to go back to sleep, back into the dream, to finish the unfinished dream, but it didn't work. I failed night after night, as if the door had closed and I wasn't allowed in any more.
For weeks, the dream stayed with me and affected my whole being. I couldn't stop thinking about it and its meaning, the burning, the longing, the desperation.
Night after night I tried to return but it didn't work. I fell into a deep depression, thinking that no one would ever understand what I had experienced that night.
My change of mood and behaviour didn't go unnoticed and one day my mum took me aside, "Julie, what's wrong with you? You hardly eat or speak. You look sad all the time. What is wrong?"
I hesitated to speak to her about my dream and knew the importance that it had for me.
"I had this dream…a dream about this castle and I don't know, I need to find it…if not I don't know what will happen."
She looked at me, irritated, "I am sure it will soon fade away and you can return to your normal state of being. Just don't give it too much thought, it was just a dream."
It was more than a dream, I knew that. This dream came from a place of high urgency, I had to find this castle no matter what. I would not let this go – I had to find this place I had seen in my dream. A part inside of me knew that this place existed and I just had to find it.

For the next fifteen years, I read every book, watched every TV program, series, any movie I could find that might include big buildings, castles or manor houses. I spent all my pocket money on my search, with no success. When I was sixteen, I convinced my parents to let me travel to

Scotland with my partner at that time. Unfortunately, I didn't find what I was looking for. But something inside of me knew that it did exist and I would find it.

Over the years, I thought maybe the castle was a symbolic meaning for something and if I were to find the right place, I would have this feeling again and would know what it was. So I started to travel all over the world and stayed in monasteries, churches and temples. I visited places of power and meaning, shared my thoughts with priests, Buddhist monks, spiritual teachers, artists, philosophers and free thinkers. All of them had interesting answers, but still it wasn't what I was looking for. My parents thought I was crazy or obsessed, other people in my town called me mad and shook their head about my idea of finding what had made me feel like this on that night.

Till one day in 2010, it was nearly fifteen years after I had my dream and I was on another trip around the world. I was spending some time in Canada, deep down in British Columbia near the Rocky Mountains. The universe did hear my calling and by accident I met Tyler. He was a Canadian guy in his mid-20s, just like me, and I felt immediately that we were connected. He knew more than others, he felt more than others and was about to reveal something to me that would change my life forever. One evening, Tyler and I decided to go for a walk and found a nice bench on top of a hill where we could overlook the Kootenay Valley. It was a clear, warm night and the stars were shining brightly. We talked about important political matters and how the world needed to change.

Suddenly Tyler turned to me and said, "What made you come here Julie? I mean all the way from Germany? Why here and why now?"

I looked into his eyes, "I am searching for something…"

"You are searching for something? What are you searching for?" He wanted to know.

I told him about my dream, about my journey and my quest to find this castle, even if it would be the last thing I did. "Do you think I am crazy? Am I wasting my time?"

He looked at the stars, "No, you are not crazy. Not at all. I know what you are looking for…"

I couldn't believe my ears, he knew what I was looking for? "What? What is it Tyler? Tell me, because I really don't know any more…!"

Tyler smiled at me, he put his hand onto his chest. "It's in here, isn't it?"

"Yes, this is exactly where I feel it. It is so strong and I don't know what it is and no one can tell me."

"It's your Soul, Julie. You are looking for your Soul. And I know that you will find your castle!"

"My Soul? Wow….is this how it feels?"
"Yes, this is exactly how it feels! You need to keep trusting in what you feel. It will show you the way."
"But I travelled all over the world, I looked in so many places and I am just not sure any more."
"You will find your castle and then you will know."
We sat there in the silence just looking at the stars, listening to the sounds around us, the birds, the water, the wind.

Mine and Tyler's path separated soon after this night and I had to travel further to New Zealand, Hong Kong and back to Germany. I treasured his words deep down in my heart. Just a few months later, when the old "German-depression" hit me again, I suddenly came across a book about spiritual healing. I had always been interested in spiritual matters such as Astrology and Philosophy, but spiritual healing was not one of them. Furthermore I was brought up by very down-to-earth German parents and there was no space for mediums or energy healing. But this could change now. I had read nearly half way through the book when I came across a story about a medium who worked at the Arthur Findlay College in England.

When I read these words something inside of me started burning, rumbling, moving – I jumped to my computer and logged into the Internet. I had to find out more about this Arthur Findlay College. When the website loaded up in front of me, my heart stopped for a moment. I was shocked, my body started to shake. What I saw there was the perfect resemblance of the castle/manor house I had in my dream when I was eleven years old. I nearly fell off my chair when I started crying. I cried for hours and hours – how was this possible? After fifteen years (I was twenty-six at that time) of restless travelling, searching, so many painful and disappointing moments – this should be it?
I had to go there and without wasting any time I booked myself a ticket to England. In February 2011, for my twenty-seventh birthday, I was on my way to the Arthur Findlay College. When I stood in front of the building I felt really dizzy and overwhelmed, tears started to run down my cheeks. I couldn't believe that I was really here. I opened the door and walked in, scenes like in a déjà vu flashed before my eyes. "I remember this place…!" The smell, the view...Oh my God...I felt like fainting any minute. I walked through the hallway like a drunkard in a dream.

Suddenly I heard Tyler's voice whispering to me, "I told you! You will find your castle!"

I looked at the view through the massive windows into the garden and I felt so much at home.

One of the staff walked past and I asked her, "Excuse me, do you know if there is any lake around here!"

She smiled at me and said, "Yes there is, you can't see it from here but if you walk down from the front door and turn left, where the big trees are, there is a small fishing lake."

My body froze, was that really true? I ran out the front door, turned left at the big trees and there was the lake. I walked around it and suddenly found myself at an angle to clearly see the Manor House from here. It started to rain and I felt like I was standing in the exact same position as I was in my dream.

How little did I know about my own psychic abilities and precognition dreams and how my life would change from here.

*The famous Stansted Hall, formerly Stansted Castle, 1871*
*Today's Arthur Findlay College (a)*

# Introduction – A Simple Structure to Spiritual Development

*"We have to dare to be ourselves, however frightening or strange that self may prove to be."*
- Mary Sarton -

Waking up to your spiritual potential is something that will go against most of what you have been taught or learnt from parents, teachers and society. It is a big step in the direction of claiming who you really are and becoming who you were meant to be.
Now is the time in which we need to acknowledge the power that lies inside of us, to be fully awake and change the way that things are heading at this moment in time.

What you have been taught about life in the current social and cultural way of upbringing has done great damage to humanity and to our planet. It seems that we have lost our way and are slowly beginning to realize that we are moving in the wrong direction.
Most of us have been denying our true, inner potential and the power that comes with it.

Many have been taught that life is a straight line that runs from A to B and all that we need to do is to make it successfully from one point to the other. If we view life as this limited, linear and temporary concept it becomes an enemy. Something that needs to be overcome or to make it through. The unpredictable is not understood as a chance but something to be avoided. Slowly we become comfortable with the illusion that we only need to do as we are told and if not then something bad will happen.

Once you start out on the spiritual path these concepts will no longer serve you. You will be asked to look for new ways of guidance.

As you awake to the spiritual dimensions, suddenly we enter a world with different laws than the logical, linear, mind-orientated creation we have been living in for the last thousands of years.
How many of you have struggled with the point of view that your life is a straight line? How many times did you feel like a failure because you wanted to go from A to B but somehow ended up at C? How many times did you blame yourself that you are not good enough because you can't compete with others or you didn't make it to the top?

And how many times did you move forward and suddenly something came in the way and pushed you right back where you started?

Our ideas of success and defeat are deeply ingrained into our cultural and social upbringing. From an early age, we have been taught to think logically and not trust in our feelings. To get a well-paid job rather than become an artist or pursue our true dreams.

This kind of thinking has destroyed our self-belief and taken away our true power, our potential and our dreams. Forced into a system that doesn't have time for new ideas or self-exploration.

Now it's time to change this and choose the path that is right for you!

> **"The intuitive mind is a sacred gift and the rational mind is a faithful servant. We have created society that honours the servant and has forgotten the gift."**
> **- Albert Einstein -**

The spiritual path is very unique for everyone. Therefore, there is no size that fits all. However, I found that there are certain steps that can help us to gain a simple structure and understanding which will serve you well on your path.

This understanding will help you to stay confident, to be less judgemental and will encourage you to embrace personal growth at any time.

My 'concept' is based on many years of personal experience in psychic and personal development, as well as the observation of hundreds of students on their spiritual path. Through my work as a teacher, I was able to pinpoint the reasons why students struggled so much and how I could help them.

I was called to create something that will address all of these problems and guide people without an absolute authority. If you integrate this understanding then you will have a simple concept that will help you to unlock your hidden potential. Furthermore, you will stay empowered because you know what is actually happening.

Spiritual Development happens in stages and is not linear. You will be asked to go back and forth between these stages to integrate the previous knowledge learnt.

The stages are simple and are based on the universal understanding of energy. This will help you along the path of your psychic exploration and will allow you to keep an eye on self-development and spiritual growth at the same time. Spiritual success is not measured in money, nor in certificates, but in the satisfaction and purpose which you give it.

This book is made up of three parts, each of which offers individual guidance on a specific area of development. Each part will give you a clear understanding and make it easy for you to take one step at a time. You can re-read each part individually and take the tests several times as you progress along.

**The three stages are:**

1. Self-Assessment

2. Foundation

3. Advancement

This is so necessary to deepen your understanding and integrate the learning.

> "What you are is what you have been.
> What you will be is what you do now"
> - BUDDHA -

**1. Self-Assessment – Part I – Where are you right now?**

The most important ingredient on your spiritual path is knowing where you are. It is a bit like a map we need for orientation when we lose focus or get our energies caught up in things or people. Reflection and self-assessment will give you confidence and offer you time to redirect the energy to where you are heading.

You need to learn to do this yourself so that you gain a realistic understanding of where you are at. In this way, you get a clear picture of your strengths, weaknesses and the parts of you that are lacking attention. Saying that, this can change from time to time and we might fall back and forth in certain stages. This is how energy works and the more you learn about it the more you are able to control it.

This is a really important process for gaining the spiritual and personal independence that comes from spiritual growth. To take personal responsibility, but also to take back the power that we would have so easily given away to a Guru, a teacher, a priest, a celebrity, a mentor or someone else that we put on a 'golden' pedestal. Don't get me wrong, you will need a guide and a teacher who can help you on your path and who can show you how to do things, but don't let this become a dependency. Don't let the appreciation of, and words of others, become your reality and determine your self-belief and your way of thinking. Trust me, I have been there, done that and guess what – I crashed and burned!

I too gave away my power, trusted others more than myself, let their opinion determine my self-worth. I felt small and insignificant, low in self-esteem and allowed their teachings to become my truth. One day I woke up and I realized I had to break free and find myself!

I learnt that everyone and everything can be my teacher. The homeless person on the street was as much my teacher as the Guru that I visited for spiritual events.

Through honest self-assessment, self-reflection and time on your own in meditation, you will come to realise where you are and what to do next. Additionally, it offers you an important starting point for your spiritual journey.

## 2. Foundation – Part II – Understanding Psychic Experiences and Phenomena

To become good at anything you will need to learn the basics and build a solid foundation. Once you have that you will move forward with confidence, because you can always fall back on it. I can't urge people enough to build this solid foundation for their spiritual growth, to truly understand how things work. Even in psychic development there are certain laws on the ways in which things work. If you understand them properly, and put enough study and training into it, maybe one day you will be able to become a master. This is the second basic ingredient and I will try to help you with this.

I have seen so many students and the most common mistake they made was that they didn't have the basic understanding of psychic development. There are many courses and teachers out there, but still a basic concept to which we all agree is missing. This lack of common ground creates a lot of frustration, misunderstanding and confusion for people. Some people easily get lost in ideas and energies, trapped in situations and are not quite sure what they actually experience. Clarity and focus are necessary to stay grounded during your spiritual progress and integrate your experiences.

I have put together what I know from my studies in Spiritualism, Occultism, Shamanism, Parapsychology and Theosophy to find an overall basic understanding for psychic experiences and phenomena.

Therefore the second part of the book offers you a solid foundation for the exploration of psychic phenomena. Only if you understand what you experience can you actually work with it.

## 3. Advancement – Part III – Forms of Expression

This is a crucial point in your psychic development journey because you need to make a decision now. This marks the entry into a commitment to learn and to take something to the next level. Here you will need to decide what you want to do next and which direction you want to pursue more deeply.

Even though you will still go back to the basics again and again and make sure your foundation gets polished. You will have discovered different routes to take, self-assessed yourself, built a foundation and now you hear the call to do something with it.

In part III of this book, I offer you a variety of routes you could take. In doing this, I hope that your horizon opens to many forms of expression and you explore what resonates with you the most.

Once you come to the advanced state, you have the opportunity to discover new forms of spiritual expression. I truly believe this can be a rather exciting journey and I am happy to be your guide along the way.

I am confident to say that if you follow my simple concept you will know what to do next and will not waste either time or money on something that you don't want to do.

*Compass by Ylanite Coppens from Pixabay, Feb2021*

# Part I

## Take the Self-Assessment Test – To find out which Development State you are in at the moment:

I want you to be proud and confident in who you are. I also want you to catch opportunities when they present themselves and feel right for you. Furthermore, I want you to be totally honest with yourself on where you are right now. Keep in mind that where you are today is not where you will be tomorrow or next week.
You can take the test again and again and it will help you to self-assess and build a solid foundation.

As I said before – spiritual development is a cyclical route and we come through the same stages repeatedly to implement and deepen our experiences. It's not linear, it's not hierarchical and it's non-judgemental. Got that? Yes? Let's go and check in with where you are right now!

Always choose one of the following answers which resonates best with you at the moment. You will find the outcome for the test at the end of this book.

## A. Do you consider yourself:

1. Often affected by the energies of others?
2. Aware of what others go through?
3. Connected to a divine guidance?
4. Aware of your own feelings?
5. Not quite sure what you want?

## B. When something doesn't feel right:

1. You know it immediately.
2. You find it difficult to remove yourself from the situation.
3. You sometimes receive answers in your dreams.
4. You look for messages, answers, symbols and numbers.
5. You leave the situation without explaining yourself.

## C. When you are feeling low, you:

1. Withdraw and take time for yourself.
2. Find it difficult to say NO to others.
3. Ask others for help.
4. Tend to suffer in silence because you don't want to be a burden to others.
5. Take good care of yourself and find ways to honour that.

## D. What is important to you right now?

1. To meet up with friends and have a good time?
2. Spend time alone and recharge?
3. To focus on your path and development?
4. Find the right partner/relationship?
5. Dive deeper into the understanding of the universe?

### E. When you perceive information, you:

1. Have difficulties understanding what it means.
2. Receive more like a flash of pictures.
3. Know what it means – if not you sit and meditate till you get clear results.
4. Easily feel overwhelmed.
5. Get easily distracted and find it hard to get back to it.

### F. Do you think you...

1. Trust in what you feel?
2. Are able to set clear boundaries with others?
3. Sometimes feel like a victim of circumstances?
4. Take care of your diet and make sure you eat the right nutrition?
5. Feel that others often take advantage of you?

### G. What fits best for you at the moment?

1. You give up easily when something doesn't work.
2. You're not quite sure where to go from here.
3. You understand that self-discovery will take time and patience.
4. You have problems taking in new information at the moment.
5. You listen compassionately and believe what others say.

### H. In relationships, you....

1. Are able to give others space to work through their own stuff?
2. Always offer a helping hand?
3. Tend to give more than you get in return?
4. Understand that you can be affected by other people's problems?
5. Speak clearly to others about what you need?

### I. What do you need right now?

1. A good self-care weekend?
2. A hug from someone you like?
3. Answers to some important questions?
4. The resources to make your dreams come true?
5. A plan for the future?

### J. If you had the choice what would you choose?

1. To get some spiritual healing?
2. Have better boundaries with others?
3. Get a Reading off a Psychic?
4. Take a psychic development course to explore your potential?
5. Being able to switch on and off what you take on from others energetically?

*Check page 169 to calculate your points.*

# Results for Self-Assessment Test

## 1. Empath (0 – 30 points):

You are in the state of an Empath at the moment. You feel deeply and compassionately. You easily absorb the energies of others and mistake them for your own. This can lead to anxiety or a feeling of overwhelm at times. You have the tendency to put others first before your own needs. Furthermore, you have problems saying NO to others because you don't want to upset anybody. This lack of boundaries can leave you drained and exhausted at times.
When you are in this state you are not quite sure who you are and what you want. You have difficulty pointing out why you feel the way you feel.

This can lead to the feeling of helplessness and victimhood to outside circumstances. In this state it is really important to take some time off, detach yourself and do some grounding. Once you have done that – it is time to take back your power.

An Empath tries to help others by taking on their problems and in some cases even tries to solve the problems for others. This lack of energetic boundaries can lead to mental and physical problems.
However, your highly developed empathic ability makes you a good person to work in any caring or healing profession.
Others might easily take advantage of this good nature. Empaths more easily end up in toxic and co-dependency relationships in which they tend to take too much responsibility. Till the day they learn to stop being a martyr and learn compassion towards themselves.
Empathic people are often attracted to animals because they drain less of their energy.
Problems around 'injustice' are also issues an empath is very much concerned about. However, the lack of focus and power can lead to a more depressed rather than empowered state.
Any forms of toxic substances (food, pollution, clothes, cleaning material) can have a big impact on such people and can cause allergies and other imbalances. Therefore it is important that empathic people acknowledge their oversensitivity and make necessary changes.

After all, being empathic and sensitive marks the basic ingredient which is needed for any psychic awareness. It builds the foundation in becoming aware of energies and influences around us.

**Tip:**

When in the empathic state we are asked to take some time off, to cleanse and recharge our batteries. To see this as a great opportunity to take stock of a situation which affected us and find some time for self-reflection in meditation. It also offers the opportunity to become aware of your saviour complex. Moreover, it can trigger the energy towards a healthier balance with the outer world.
Establish clear boundaries, saying NO or 'Stop' when exhausted and tired is majorly important to gaining clarity in this emotionally confused state.

I created this really great exercise, inspired by Dave Markowitz the Author of *Self-Care for the Self-Aware*. Do the exercise when you are feeling overwhelmed or stuck in an empathic state.

1. Sit down for a short meditation in which you scan the whole of your body. Become aware of any tension, pains or sensations.

2. With the next breath I want you to choose the one that stands out the most. Slowly breath into this area of tension or pain. Allow it to soften with every breath you take.

3. Allow any emotions that are hiding behind the tension or the pain to come to the surface and enter into your consciousness.

4. With the next breath I want you to ask the emotions if they are yours or if you have taken them on from someone else. The first answer that comes to your mind is the right one.

If you have taken on the emotions from another person, I want you to now visualise before your inner eye the situation in which this happened. Where were you? What did you do? Who was with you and what did you speak about?

- Wait for the answer... allow it to manifest before your inner eye.

With the next breath I want you to now feel yourself right back into the original situation. Picture yourself exactly where you were back then. What did you do or say? What did the other person do or say? Become aware of the moment when you suddenly realized that something shifted.

Somehow a foreign energy entered your body or mind. If you can't get a clear picture, ask your higher self to help you.
Once you've located the moment in which the shift happened – I want you to stop there. Take a deep breath in. Look at the energy that created the shift. What have you taken on from the other person?

Their problem, pain, frustration, anger, fear, desperation. Or have you offered to take responsibility or to solve the problem out of compassion?

5. With the next breath I want you to take this energy and hold it in your hands for a moment before you give it back to the person you took it from.

Imagine how the energy leaves your body and returns to the other person.

Say thank you for the connection and visualise yourself now with golden white light all around you.

6. If the answer previously wasn't another person but yourself, you need to ask your higher self to take it away and release it.

## *FREE GIFT*

### *Get this Meditation Session "Empath Body Scan" for Free:*

Visit www.unlockingpsychicpotential.com to download it

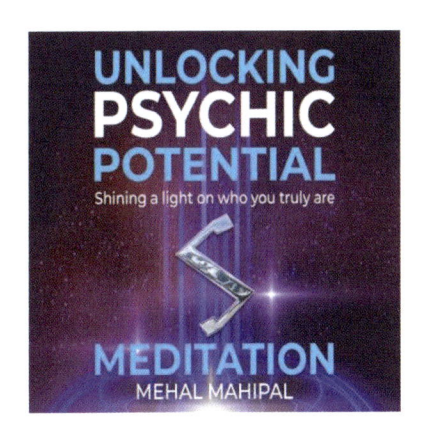

**Signs that we have taken on too much:**

- depression, anxiety, burn out, exhaustion, headaches, over thinking, unexplainable sudden pains.

What to do:

Avoid being there for others or helping them. Focus on yourself and find ways to gain new balance. Eliminate refined sugars from your diet and replace with healthy alternatives such as rice syrup, stevia, coconut sugar, fruit sugar.
Starchy and earthy foods such as carrots, butternut squash, sweet potatoes, leeks, onions etc. can be helpful to give you a feeling of nourishment and grounding.

To acknowledge your own vulnerability, as well as the awareness of changes of energetic cycles, will help you to gain more awareness. If you start paying more attention, this knowledge can slowly be integrated into your daily life.
The psychic force is very closely connected to the female menstrual cycle. Many women experience their psychic awakening around their first menstrual cycle as a teenager. Maybe this is also the reason why we see more women working in the field because their intuition is more deeply developed.

**Observing the Menstrual Cycle in more detail:**

There is an amazing book I would recommend to you for further reading on this subject, by Alexandra Pope and Sjanie Hugo Wurlitzer – *Wild Power : Discover the Magic of Your Menstrual Cycle and Awaken the Feminine Path to Power.*

It can be helpful for women to start observing their menstrual cycle. The highs and lows of their energies, as well as their needs and things to avoid during this time are very crucial.

The actual time of menstruation is a resting time in which we should allow ourselves to let go of any responsibility. Your mind is as if in another dimension and you have problems thinking logically.

| | |
|---|---|
| Days 1 – 5 | The nervous system repairs itself and we need to slow down and rest. |
| Days 6 – 11 | Women are more tolerant and energetic and can take on more. |
| Days 12 (ovulation) – 18 | Most women are full of energy and feel like they are on the top of the world. |
| Days 19 – 21 | The game changes and we enter a very critical phase → changeover day. The hormones drop and we can experience a short time of mood swings or depression. We experience zero tolerance towards others. We tend to be much more critical and want to get stuff done. |
| Days 28/29 | A very critical point just before menstruation. Often marked with emotional crisis, rage or anger, even suicidal thoughts sometimes until the bleed starts. |

This knowledge can really help you to understand how you actually operate and allows you to look after yourself more or to look after others at the right time. It puts things into perspective and also makes you aware of which times you are more sensitive and why.

It is time to start your own menstrual journal.
Suddenly, what we perceived as limitations, shortcomings and failures can be understood as life-enhancing, inbuilt survival modes.
**Self-help:**

Detox regularly with bath salts (Epsom/Magnesium/Himalayan) as this helps to wash away negative energies which you have taken on.
Introduce non-toxic cleansing materials for house and body.
Start observing the seasons and the moon cycle, and feel how your energy differs with the changes.

**Space Clearing Sprays:**
Empaths can be so easily affected by other people's energies. For this reason, you could consider one of our Space Clearing Sprays to remove any negative energy in your environment. While our Psychic Protection Sprays will offer you energetic protection when dealing with others. The sprays are made with high quality essential oils, colloidal silver and gold, shamanic and flower essences.

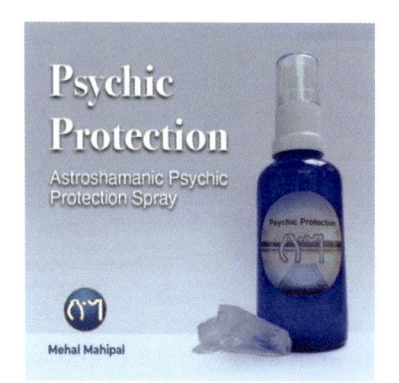

*You can find both of them in our online shop at www.mehalmahipal.com*

## **Be mindful:**

We often fall back into the state of an Empath because we have an inborn desire to help others. Once this sense is triggered, we can go beyond our boundaries. Especially if someone who is close to us experiences a crisis, we tend to sacrifice our own energetic balance to help them.

Another time we might be stuck in an old belief system or an old trauma is triggered. This can lead to a complete, sudden energetic openness and vulnerability. It's important to acknowledge when this happens, especially during your training in psychic abilities, and take good care of yourself till you have found stable ground again.
You will come back to the state of an Empath many times over and each time you will learn deeper lessons about yourself and others. Appreciate the times when you feel oversensitive and act accordingly.

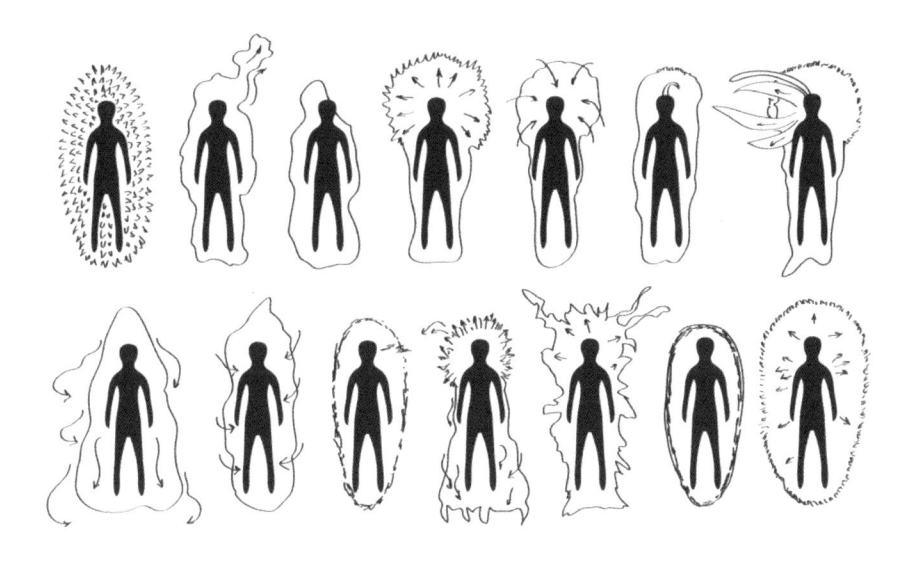

*(b) The auric field and its many forms of emotional expression*

Here are two short exercises for you to do which will teach you more about the empathic state:


**1. Exercise – The Energy of Thought Forms**

For this exercise you will need another person. It would be best if you had someone who you don't know that much about. If not, take whoever is available.
Sit back to back with each other – take a piece of paper and a pen and for ten minutes both of you write down what you feel, think etc.
After ten minutes, turn around and face each other.
Now share what you have written down, one after the other and see what is yours and what actually belongs to the other person and you have mistaken it as your own thoughts or feelings.
This is a great exercise to make you aware about energy and thought forms.

**This exercise will help you to gain more objectivity and not identify so much with your feelings.**




**2. Exercise – The Observer**

Observe how you feel before and after you get on a train or bus.
Sit down next to someone or close to them, and observe how you feel now and what your thoughts are.
Stand up and grab another seat and observe how you feel now.

Do you now understand how you can be affected by energy and by other people's thoughts and feelings?

## 2. Intuitive (31 – 45 points):

The state of the Intuitive resonates with you the most at the moment. You are aware of synchronicity and the basics of energy. You are in touch with your intuition and you have a sense of what feels right or wrong. You can easily see through other people, you can even feel if someone is toxic.

An Intuitive is a deep thinker and questions a lot of things that seem to be normal to other people. Often, such people have an interest in spiritual and holistic matters and feel drawn to natural medicine and holistic therapies.
Most intuitive people are aware of the connection of body, mind and spirit. At this stage, your need to connect with like-minded people is stronger than that of the Empath.
Therefore, it would be good for you to keep an eye out for development courses and groups. Your desire to explore your own potential could lead you in the direction of healing, counselling or natural therapies, as well as the paranormal or spiritual studies.
Even though you feel drawn to these areas, you might lack a bit of direction or clarity as to what would suit you best. The creative arts, music and other inspiratory hobbies could help you expand your horizon and allow you to connect to the underlying currents of spiritual energy.

At the intuitive state you seek deeper meaning and purpose in your life. Something inside of you is telling you that there is much more than meets the eye.
However, you have not fully developed enough awareness yet regarding this inner guidance. Your lack of confidence and faith in your abilities makes you hesitant at times. In relationships, you might feel as if someone is toxic but you still find it difficult to act accordingly. A part of yourself is still sacrificing for the sake of others. This can lead to inner tension at times with feelings of guilt, shame, frustration and anger.

The best way to gain more clarity and structure on these matters would be to start slowly working on yourself. Uncovering the deeply buried feelings inside of you and making them conscious thoughts. If you sought some guidance from a counsellor or therapist, that could be of great support to you.
At this point there is also some work to do with things that have happened in the past and still have power over you.

Highlighting these areas in which we still hold grudges, are unable to forgive, are holding on to things or are energetically tied to unresolved issues, can help us to become clear. Otherwise you will not free yourself from past wounds and you will be unable to truly step into your power.
Taking stock and self-assessing situations in which you feel blocked can be beneficial.

Meditation can offer a safe space to check in with oneself. By doing this, you will gain objectivity and see other people as they are. Many of those other people actually serve as mirrors to point out all the things that we should look at in ourselves.
The more you trust in what you feel and act accordingly without overthinking or doubting it – the stronger your psychic force will become.

Becoming aware of where you may be lacking, your own weaknesses and shortcomings, is not an easy process and requires a gentle approach. Sometimes it can be helpful to ask a professional healer to help us with this. Additionally, self-assessment means to become aware of who you want to be and what you have already accomplished. Often at this stage we admire people (or fall in love with them) who possess or represent something that we would like to have. This can be a personality trait, a certain look, an achievement, a material possession or anything else. Just another form of projection which is not based on trauma (past) but (future) potential.
Such relationships are often energetically unbalanced and, in many cases, won't last. Once we acquire what we needed (to learn), the person suddenly disappears.
If we want a balanced (energetically) relationship we will need to become aware what (who) we would like to be and try to give this to ourselves. By doing so we will also attract someone who will love us for who we are and support our endeavours.

In the intuitive state we are much more open to divine guidance and synchronicity. We look for signs and patterns that confirm our intuitive feeling. There is nothing wrong with that and it can be quite a magical and exciting phase – To see how everything is confirming what we feel. However the universal law of resonance states: "The energy flows where attention goes" and we want to become aware of this. True power lies inside of us and all you need to know is already there.
The signs we see are confirming what we feel and can be really helpful at times.

There are many ways in which the universe speaks to us and lets us know that we are loved and supported. Trust that!

**Next steps for an Intuitive:**

1. Learn to act on your intuition
2. Try to make more decisions based on intuition
3. Take charge
4. Challenge your intuition in everyday life (What to eat? What do you need right now?)
5. Energetically scan your friends and family circle and assess how they make you feel and why.
6. Take our Self Study Course 'UNLOCKING YOUR PSYCHIC POTENTIAL'.

(c) *The Intuitive is aware of a higher power moving through her*

## 3. Awakened Intuitive (46 – 65 points):

This state or stage represents your full awareness of your powers. You have the ability to set clear boundaries and you are confident to speak the truth as well as to trust your inner judgement.
This person is confident about their inner guidance and is able to say NO to others. You also ask actively for help if you need it.
The confusion of the first two states is gone and here you can see much more clearly. You are striving to unfold your potential and understand spiritual awakening as a direction in life. Your heightened self-awareness and the work you did on yourself is finally paying off.
You are not afraid of your power and you are familiar with the idea that actions have consequences. This leads to making healthy choices and through them you allow yourself to grow. Many people in this state practice yoga or other forms of energy movement. They look after their diet, include necessary supplements and take regular time out to recharge and rest.
In this state we know how energy works, as well as its effects on well-being and we often experiment with Tarot Cards, Healing, Psychic Development and look into Astrology.
The Awakened Intuitive is more empowered than the Intuitive and takes more action. You are aware of your own shadow and know that you can project your own hopes, fears and shortcomings onto others.

In this state it's much easier to look through people or things without losing our own objectivity.
The Awakened Intuitive person has gone through phases of loneliness and gained resilience and inner strength from it. These insights act as a catalyst to become aware of the innermost power as a tool for transformation and self-discovery.

The Awakened Intuitive is more aware if their body, mind and spirit is out of balance and also senses whether it is energetic attachments which are causing this. Actively he/she finds ways to release these on a regular basis to bring back the harmony of body, mind and spirit.

The Awakened Intuitive trusts in the inner guidance even against all odds and can overcome great obstacles. In this energetic state we take time to heal ourselves instead of giving too much to others.
You are striving to unfold your own potential and seek ways to express yourself authentically.

Trauma is made conscious through therapy, self-reflection and assessment, as well as in healing sessions. Accepting their own limitations without feeling bad about it is a virtue the Awakened Intuitive is aspired to achieve.

The Awakened Intuitive is not only aware of the signs from the divine, but also knows that he/she can learn from anyone or any situation. Most people in this state actively work with the Law of Attraction and consciously focus on elevating their vibrational frequency.

It is different to the empathic state in which we always want to help others no matter how we feel or whether we have the energetic resources. The awakened intuitive knows that we can't interfere in someone else's karma and sometimes this means that we help others by not directly helping them.

This state is the most empowered state of the three and here we no longer tolerate toxic relationships, friendships or situations that makes us sick. In this state we consciously apply energetic protection, space clearing and recharge our batteries when we are low. An Awakened Intuitive can sense the difference between a needy person (who often drains our energy and actually doesn't want to change) and someone who is willing to change. Based on this understanding, the Awakened Intuitive will give their energy, time etc. accordingly.

An Awakened Intuitive is aware of the energetic influence of his/her ancestors (DNA), past lives and how they can have an impact on our personal development.

Past life regression, tracing their own lineage and releasing what is not beneficial and has been passed down from previous generations, can be of major help in progressing forward.

Hypnotherapy offers the opportunity to enter into different states of consciousness whilst in a safe environment. This could be a good way to uncover deeper lying truth. Of course, this will depend on the quality of the therapist you work with.

The universal laws become more relevant and their study and understanding can add great value to your path.

d) *Woman meditating*

It is impossible to only be in one of the three states all the time. This is really important to understand because otherwise we will get frustrated about our own expectations. Realistically, if we are just starting out on our spiritual journey, we will be bouncing between the first two states. Then, after a few years of work on ourselves and more training, our understanding deepens and we reach the Awakened Intuitive state. However, we will still experience a return to the empathic state at times, especially when we are low on energy and our boundaries are not really clear. Additionally, when something really triggers our heart space, we more easily forget about the principles of energy and how they affect us.

Nevertheless, it is totally fine to find ourselves moving between these states and even more important to know when we are experiencing problems. This simple concept of the three states of energy awareness can help you as a guideline to check in with where you are right now and offers practical solutions on how to help yourself.

**Next Steps:**

- Start regularly SITTING IN THE POWER ( a powerful meditation practice which helps you to   build spiritual power – will be taught in the 'UNLOCKING YOUR PSYCHCIC POTENTIAL' COURSE)
- Start journaling dreams/experiences (visions)
- Start using Tarot Cards for Healing
- Start looking more into Healing, Blessings, Psychic Work and development opportunities
- Start developing your clair senses more actively
- Fine tune your dietary habits
- Practice yoga, breathing exercises, qi-gong etc.
- Practice meditation for the higher states of consciousness
- Take our Self Study Course 'UNLOCKING YOUR PSYCHIC POTENTIAL'.

*(e) The Awakened Intuitive combines intuition with personal strength*

## **Why develop your psychic abilities?**

In our modern world full of new technologies and consumerism we are slowly drifting away from who we truly are. Furthermore, we get so absorbed and eaten up by distractions that we are actually losing touch with what makes us human.
Shaped by a culture that values profit over people and time over meaning we have reached a crucial turning point in our evolution.
Bombarded by the opinion of mass media and influenced by social media, it becomes more and more difficult to remain a critical thinker. I understand that progress needs to be made and nature does it all the time. However, this should be along the lines of 'let's not forget who we truly are and what we came here for'.
A spiritual soul experiencing a physical body with all its limitations and pleasures. While the body is trapped in space and time and one day will cease to exist – the soul does not. The soul will continue its journey to discover more of itself.
The more the soul recognises itself, the more it will be able to grow and transform. By developing your psychic potential you honour the soul's longing to understand itself.
And the more you start out on your spiritual journey, the more you will remember that we all have infinite potential inside of us. This was given to us by the universe, which moves in us and through us.
The psychic force which moves inside of you is the life-long connection to the place where you once came from.

Once we are born into a physical body many of us forget about this itinerant gift and deny our true spiritual nature. Those people have difficulty finding purpose and meaning while here on earth.
They will try many things and still don't feel that it is quite right. I know this feeling very well, I have been there myself. I allowed others to tell me what to do because I didn't know better. Till one day I touched upon something inside of me that was so different from anything else I had ever felt before. On this day, I realised that I would not rest unless I could give this something a name and find out what it was that made me feel this way. So, I started out on my very own soul's path that led me all over the world in many different directions and to meet many different people. All of them added a little piece to this puzzle which I was trying to solve. I overcame obstacles that stood in my way and reached a point of total transformation. Sometimes it was difficult and hard, doubts suddenly stood in the road, voices of other people who thought they knew better. Old conditioning came up and I was confronted with my limiting beliefs.

However, only by expanding my mind, staying focused and following this inner voice that was guiding me, was I able to discover my real super powers. My spiritual gifts are God given and so are yours. They were planted inside of me long before my feet touched the earth. Once I acknowledged the real potential inside of me, doors started to open and healing took place.

I want to invite you to dare to go on this journey, on your very own soul's path. By discovering the light within you, the shadow of separation will disappear. You will gain confidence in who you are and what you came here for. The opinion of others will not be important any more when you start living the truth that comes from inside of you. When you start creating a more spiritual life things suddenly will fall into place and the connection with the divine will become a guiding light in your personal life. You will discover the power of self-healing and the deep satisfaction of healing others. Your mind will expand and thought transference, psychometry, the ability to dream your life into being, communication without words and clear knowing are just some of the expressions you might gain. Furthermore, once you connect with what is inside of yourself you are all that – all that you always have been. You not only become a better person but the world becomes a better place.

*Spiritual Awakening by Okan Caliskan, Pixabay Feb 2021*

# PART II

## 2.1. What are Psychic Abilities and Why do We have Them?

*"It's only with the heart that one can see rightly,
what is essential is invisible to the eye"*
**- Antoine de Saint-Exupery -**

Everybody was given an infinite spiritual potential which goes far beyond the physical limitations. This potential is often deeply hidden inside of us and has been pushed back and suppressed by years of social and cultural conditioning. It is time to unlock this Soul Potential and uncover who you truly are.

When you were born into this world (once again) you brought with you the memories of the place you initially came from. Deep inside of you there is still this glimpse, this knowing, that there is so much more than the eyes can see. There are many children who remember and speak about past lives. Some of them give astonishing details about the place where they lived another life, details on how they passed and what they have done before. These memories are the last evidence about an infinite force that goes beyond logical thinking. Something that is far greater than the 'normal' mind wants us to believe.
These records can be found all over the world and we can't deny the fact that we might have lived other lives before. The reason for this could be that to completely grow into our full potential we might need to incarnate several lifetimes to grow and experience the physical world.
The older we get, the more we tend to forget about our past experiences and no longer remember where we once came from. Most children have very vivid memories about past lives till the age of seven years. The time where school education and social conditioning start interfering. By the age of thirteen, most of the memories of past lives are lost and hardly accessible for the conscious mind.
On my personal journey, I remembered my past life very clearly, it was so vivid and real to me that I could not deny it. Even though other people thought I might have lost the plot, I always knew that I was right and carried this deep down in my heart.

Our minds are conditioned by our social, cultural and parental upbringing. Additionally teachers, religions, society and the government contribute to 'helping' us settle into this life.

Many of us get so caught up in the survival of the physical body that we totally forget or deny our spiritual inheritance. However, there is a part inside of us that will never forget and will keep reminding us in many ways. The soul cannot die and consciousness will move on to the next plane after physical death.

Even if we are sent to school, followed by going to college or university, get a job, fall in love, get married, have children and so on, at a certain point in our lives we will encounter an experience that will trigger something inside of us. The psychic force will make itself heard to put us straight back on the right track. Some of these experiences can be rather disturbing – break ups, job loss, divorce, death of a loved one or a serious illness. Suddenly we remember that physical life is only temporary and doesn't always work out as planned.

Once we hit such 'turning points', we often fall into a search for meaning. This is when the spiritual awakening takes place.

Most of these people will be pushed towards the path of truth – one way or the other – and this time can be very confusing and painful.

Suddenly they feel the urge to explore the questions, 'What else is there? Who are we if we lose everything? What comes after this life and where do we go from here?'

The more we ask, the more we eventually gain answers and these answers will challenge our current belief system and take us out of our comfort zone.

I remember clearly the time when I was going through a massive spiritual awakening (and I had thought that I was already very spiritual) when I first received a message from a Spiritualist Medium at the Arthur Findlay College.

Ashley Wright, the medium who gave me a message from my grandmother, had worked at the College for quite a while. Following in his parents', and grandparents' footsteps, who were always involved with Stansted Hall even before it became a College. His demonstration of mediumship changed my life forever.

When I sat at the Arthur Findlay College in February 2011 for the first time ever, I still felt raw and vulnerable and was dealing with my grief. My grandmother had passed away just two years prior to the moment I found myself sitting in the audience of 150 people at a public Spiritualist Service. Never had I been to such a service before, nor did I know much about mediums.

Ashley started to speak about an elderly lady who was with him, small, well-built and with a good sense of humour. He said that this lady was not from the UK but he knew that she had visited London once and enjoyed that very much. Ashley described a house with a thatched roof which was very common for the area in which she used to live.

He also said that the lady suffered from heart problems, her husband had died many years ago, that he passed away in a hospital within three days and it was very unexpected. Two people in the audience raised their hands because they understood what the medium said, I just kept listening. But I felt something inside of me that made me rather uncomfortable.

Ashley wasn't convinced that he was with the right person so he continued, "I know this lady goes by the name Mary and she is looking for her granddaughter".

In this moment, I felt that a lightning bolt had just hit me. I knew it was for me and tears ran down my cheek. My friend who sat next to me pointed their finger at me and someone passed me the microphone to confirm with the medium. I was shocked and just wanted to run out of the room, rather than having 150 people staring at me while I was crying my eyes out. I could hardly speak, "Yes, it is my grandmother I think."

The medium smiled at me, "She was very determined to find you!"

I tried to smile with my teary eyes and felt my heart nearly breaking again – I missed her so much. The medium mentioned about shared memories, how I visited her in hospital and she was already unconscious but she knew I was there. "Oh gosh, she loves that you are here today and she says that all this is so exciting! She is really pleased that you finally found your castle. I don't know what that means but she said you know."

People started laughing and even I spared a smile. My grandmother knew about my 'obsession' to find my castle one day and I couldn't believe that this came up on this day. Everything the medium said was one hundred percent accurate and really blew my mind.

When the service was over, I had to ground myself. I had difficulties digesting and realizing what had just happened. I mean, how was this possible? Why now?

For days I sat down and couldn't get my head around what had happened. I even called my parents and told them about my experience – they probably thought that I had now totally lost my mind.

It marked a huge turning point in my life, the knowledge that there is so much more than the eyes can see. This experience also opened me up to discovering my spiritual gifts and finally let healing take place from all the grief I held inside. I felt that I cracked open. I was spinning between nervous breakdown and thoughts of, "what if I have lost my mind now?" It took me a few days to find common ground again.

After this experience I needed to come back to the College and find out more about all this. That week I went to another lecture about Mediumship but this time it was held in the library of the AFC. I clearly couldn't get enough of these experiences and soaked them up like a sponge. When the lecture was over and all the people left the room, I spent some time by myself in the room. While I was looking around, I suddenly heard a voice (clairaudient) saying, "Julie, one day you will be standing here on stage with these other mediums!"

My heart was pounding. Me? On Stage? In front of all the other people? With my anxiety, low self-esteem and nervous tension? I clearly don't think so! – I said to myself. Little did I know back then how right this little spirit voice was. Something inside of me shifted and I felt that after all these years in which I was looking, searching, asking, I had finally arrived home.

Your psychic potential was given to you for a reason, so that you are able to live a more purposeful and meaningful life. Furthermore, it enables you to discover talents, gifts and support that otherwise would not have been accessible to you.

Psychic Development is the first step towards discovering your Soul's path. Realizing your own potential and trusting that you have got so much more to learn.

## Psychic Powers

The psychic force is the energy that pushes you forward to fulfil your mission in life. This force is directed by the divine universe and its translator is your soul. Your soul understands the secret working of energy and vibrations which enable it to receive impressions that go beyond the physical. It is unconsciousness made conscious if you will, while your intuition is the key to directing this force.
This psychic force, or soul energy, can be studied and better understood through the psychic senses. If those are well trained and developed it opens us up to other dimensions which are not visible to the naked eye. They are not tangible to the physical touch and they are not limited by space and time.

Every living organism is nourished by the universal life force that gives life to all that is. Once the life force is cut off – physical death appears. However the psychic force continues to exist far beyond the physically deceased. Consciousness cannot die. Even animals are aware of the psychic force but on a much more instinctual level than humans are. They are able to sense energies, danger, love etc. but they lack the gift of self-awareness. This doesn't mean animals are not intelligent rather that they are not aware of themselves as much as we humans are. They eat when hungry, sleep when tired and react with fight or flight mode when threatened. They react. We as humans have the ability to reflect on our own and other's behaviour. We are able to understand cause and effect and we are aware that our physical existence is only temporary. This means we perceive space and time as limitation on a physical level. However, the awareness of the psychic force allows us to go beyond these limitations. Similar to animals who have certain heightened senses such as dogs (smell), eagles (seeing), cats (hearing) etc. we are also given the ability to heighten our awareness to a certain degree.
This allows us to see, hear, feel things that are on a much finer frequency than the physical. For example: "A mother can sense that her child is not well or is in danger even if the child is hundreds of miles away." This clearly shows us that the psychic force (soul energy) can overcome space and time.

This mother's instinct is a great example of the soul connection with other beings. The mother only 'knows' that something is not right but can't tell exactly what it is. We understand this in psychic development as the basic level of psychic power, which is intuition without clear knowing. We all have this to a certain degree, especially with people we

are closely connected with. Some people even sense world events before they are actually happening. Others might be able to sense if someone is going to die, but most of them don't know when or how (maybe that is a good thing).
There are people who can see people who just passed away without knowing that they actually passed. I will talk about this in more detail later in this book.

The more we become aware of our soul energy, the more we will be pushing the boundaries of the so-called known.
It is very easy to get lost or confused in such experiences and only structure and knowledge will help you to understand them. Furthermore, it will help you to develop a certain degree of your psychic powers safely. Psychic development will not only blow your mind but will change your whole world view forever.
It will liberate you from what you were told to be and allow you to become who you actually are.
Over the years I have seen so many people on this path and have witnessed their transformation. Discovering your own soul potential and your gifts can be one of the most interesting journeys you will ever take.
In the next chapters I want to offer you some structure on your path, so that you gain confidence in the person you will become.

*Believe in Yourself by Muhammad Haseeb, Pixabay, Feb2021*

# 2.2 – The Clair Senses

## Clairvoyance or Extra Sensory Perception (ESP)

The clair senses are the heightened version of our normal senses, they allow us to be able to become aware of things which are made of finer energetic frequency. The ability to perceive such impressions or information through these psychic channels is latent in everybody. Some people have a heightened natural awareness of these senses by birth. Others can achieve these or similar levels through the right development and training. However, both of them need to be rightly trained to be able to master them.

### The Basic Clair Senses are:

1. Clairvoyance    clear seeing
2. Clairaudience    clear hearing
3. Clairsentience    clear sensing → clearly knowing (mastery)
4. Clairscent    clear smelling
5. Clairgustance    clear tasting
6. Clairtangency    clear touch (also known as Psychometry)

In the next chapters, I'll explain each of these senses in more detail. This will enable you to understand the clair senses more clearly, as well as their expression and phenomena. They are an important part of being able to build a solid foundation of knowledge.

*(f) Recent psychic evidence by Arthur Conan Doyle, New York Times 1923*

# Clairvoyance:

The ability to 'see' things with the 'inner' eye or the 'etheric' eye. The most important ingredient to expanding one's ability in this area is to have a good imagination. People who have a good imagination often have fewer problems developing this faculty. Over many years of personal development and seeing hundreds of students developing their abilities, I came to realize that there is a difference between the developmental stages and different genders. Women possess a more naturally strongly developed intuition and their brain is totally differently wired which makes it easier for them to perceive clairvoyant impressions. Men, however, experience much more difficulty in accessing this ability. This would also explain the phenomena of the 'mother's instinct' which I spoke about before. The mother needs to 'know' or be 'aware' of her child's needs, especially during the early stages when verbal communication of the child is limited. This clearly shows that nature gave women a heightened sense of intuition.

Nonetheless, it doesn't mean that men can't develop outstanding clairvoyant abilities. I simply wish to say that men need different ways to do that. In my personal and professional opinion, I think that men and women need different exercises or training units to develop clairvoyance due to the different structure of their brains.

Clairvoyance differs widely in character and degree. It can depend upon whether a person is trained, untrained, under mesmeric influence, independent or in an exercise. Some people experience clairvoyance in an awakened state that includes their physical body. Other people have such experiences when they are asleep or in a trance state. Only with the right training and development is it possible to bring clairvoyance under the influence of the will and make the right interpretations.

Clairvoyance can appear in different phenomena and I would like to give you a few examples that might shed some light on your personal experiences.

1. Psychic Vision and Mediumship
2. Visions and Prophecies (Precognition)
3. Apparitions
4. Telepathy & Mind Reading
5. Ghosts and Spirits.

# 1. Psychic Vision and Mediumship

Both of these forms require the ability to become aware of things with the 'inner' eye. I think that there is still some massive confusion about these abilities and how they are perceived in mainstream understanding.

**Psychic Vision:**

A Psychic Medium receives information from a person's energy field and by blending with the person's soul. This can express itself through colours, pictures or some kind of vision. They can give information about a person's past, present and future potential. This is based on the understanding that everything we have ever experienced is stored in our auric field (the etheric body). A Psychic is not able to predict the future. Anybody who says they could is clearly lying and not aware of their own abilities and their limitations. The future is not set in stone, but is rather an accumulation of choices we make in the present moment.
A Psychic Reading can be of true spiritual guidance if the Psychic Medium is trained well and knows what they are doing. By 'seeing' what others can't see, it offers great potential to see certain things from a different perspective. How often are we standing in our own way and we just can't see clearly?

To train your psychic vision is not only of interest for those of you who actually want to give psychic readings. It is also utterly helpful in so many areas. Just imagine a doctor had been trained in psychic vision and could therefore understand much more about his/her patients' actual problems. What about a police officer or firefighter with psychic vision – would that not help much better in solving crimes if they could see danger before it actually happens?
Imagine a school teacher with psychic vision, he/she could see both real potential or possible struggles in students and could help and support much more sufficiently. What about yoga teachers, or people who work with people with disabilities? A nurse trained in psychic vision might be able to give better medication and better care because she understands or sees the effects of the medication on her patients much more easily. What about lawyers with psychic visions? The list could go on and on and on.

Check out the famous Psychic, Edgar Cayce – he helped thousands with his ability to diagnose people in his sleep. He was even able to tell people what they needed in order to heal and recover fully. More than 8,000 of Cayce's 14,306 readings were given for individuals suffering from various ailments. He often asked these clients to also consult with professional healthcare providers of the time, and Cayce himself worked with a number of different doctors when giving his health readings. The Edgar Cayce Health Database is a wonderful encyclopaedia of health information.

You can find out more here: www.edgarcayce.org

*(g)Young Edgar Cayce – picture in the public domain.*

It is so important that psychic development is a door-opener and often we are not quite sure where we are heading. Edgar Cayce is a great example, as he started by doing health readings and later on was called to offer psychic surgery too.
We can't force the direction of our spiritual progress, but we can start to explore our potential.

**Have you ever had a psychic vision? Did you somehow intuitively know what the other person was going through, where their pain was located? Mediumship:**

"The receipt of information not available through the normal senses, ostensibly from spirits of the dead or gods. Besides serving as a conduit for communication between the living and the world beyond, mediums may heal and produce physical phenomena, such as movement of objects and the control of the weather (see Psychokinesis.)
Mediums have been known by various names, among them oracle, soothsayer, wizard, cunning woman, fortune-teller, witch, wise woman, witch doctor, medicine man, sorcerer, shaman, mystic, priest, prophet and channeller. However, distinctions are also often made between these

terms. According to anthropologist Michael Winckelmann, the role of the medium – and of several other magico-religious practitioner types – developed historically out of the shaman. The origins of modern mediumship began in research of mesmerism during the 19th century. Some subjects who were "magnetized," or hypnotized, fell under the control of spirits and delivered messages from the Other Side. Like shamans who communicate with the spirit world by becoming possessed by godlings, spirit animals, and deities, the mesmeric subjects became temporary possessed by discarnate spirits (see Spiritualism)." *Rosemary Ellen Guiley, 'Encyclopaedia of Ghosts and Spirits' page 245/246, 2001.*

## Eileen Garrett and the British Airship R101:

One of the most dramatic and unusual events in the history of the entire Spiritualist movement occurred in October 1930.

"Just two days after the huge British airship, the R101, had gone down in flames on a hillside in France --- killing 48 of its 54 passengers --- the halting voice of a man claiming to be its captain spoke through the lips of a medium in London. In short and disjointed sentences, he described his horrifying last moments before the airship burned. His account of the crash included a wealth of technical information that was not only confirmed six months later by an official inquiry, but was well beyond the knowledge of the medium delivering the message. The disaster, which occurred on October 5, 1930, claimed the lives of dozens of British citizens, including two high-ranking aviation officials. It shook the government's confidence in airships and ended the British efforts to develop these types of craft for commercial use. In short, the disaster had a devastating effect on England as a whole."

(h) *Seance Flyer Eileen Garrett*

The séance at which this dramatic communication took place occurred at the National Laboratory of Psychical Research, which had been founded by Harry Price four years earlier. Price, his secretary and journalist Ian D. Coster, had arranged a sitting with a reportedly talented young medium named Eileen Garrett. The purpose of it was to try and make contact with the spirit of Sir Arthur Conan Doyle, who had recently passed away. The report of the séance was to be published in an upcoming magazine."
(https://www.americanhauntingsink.com/garrett, 2020.)

(i) *Herbert Carmichael Irwin- AFC Flight Lieutenant Royal Air Force*

(j) *Airship R101 – in 1929*

**Did you ever receive a message from a deceased loved one? What do you think about life after death? Are you intrigued about communicating with other spheres and spirits? What would you say to your loved ones if you passed on?**

## 2. Visions and Prophecies

This is often referred to as clairvoyance in time. This marks the ability to see objects or events which are removed from the seer in time – the power of looking into the future. This is classified as a higher form of clairvoyance. It is very rare that we have such people any more, moreover there are some people who think that they can look into the future when they actually just see potential or possibilities. This happens a lot in untrained people who experience forms of psychic vision and then tell their clients about their future. Such people clearly don't understand their own level of development and don't follow any code of ethics in their work.

If you could look into the future, how would you know that what you see is actually going to happen? And if you could have this ability, do you think it would be a gift or a curse? Would you not carry a lot of responsibility?

Clairvoyance is always subject to human error and this will always be the case. Therefore, it is so important we treat this part very softly and with uttermost caution. Certainly, there have been some famous seers, or prophets in the past and if we look into their prophecies did all of them really come true?

Visions and prophecies are also more likely to occur in a trance or sleep state than in a state of psychic vision. They fall under the category of precognition and precognition dreams are probably the most known form of prophecy or visions.

If you read the beginning of my book, you will have read my story and the precognition dream I had when I was eleven years old. Of course, at that time I was not aware that I had actually perceived a vision. All I knew back then was that I had to find out about this feeling, and it took me fifteen years and travelling all around the world to find it. Back in those days, I didn't even know about psychic abilities, mediums or anything else that I have discussed here. But I trusted my intuition and I followed it wherever it took me. Looking back, this book would not have been written if all this had not happened.

Precognition dreams are a 'higher' form of clairvoyance. We find a lot of people who claim to have this ability and it is dangerous to do so when you don't know what your abilities and limitations are.

How can you be really sure that what you dream is going to happen? It could also be a part of your personal imagination or fantasy. It could be unresolved issues or experiences that you had during the day and which found their way into your dream state. It may be your personal fears or worries that have come from your subconscious mind into the conscious mind.

To claim that you have precognition dreams and tell others about it can cause great harm and end up in self-fulfilling prophecies. In such cases I am referring to 'precognition dreams' in which people might see or experience that something will happen to someone. This is to be treated with caution. As I said before, it is important to stay grounded because we often can't tell if we might be dreaming our own fears or worries.

Without regard, the ability to dream events or situations that have not yet happened is very well-known and sleeping is certainly another state of mind. This makes it easier to gain impressions that we normally would not get during the normal waking state. If you want to explore this subject further, I would suggest that you start a dream journal. In this way, you can record your dreams and see their significance over time.
This will be very beneficial towards developing awareness of your clairvoyance. You can also look out for a trained teacher or mentor who can guide you on this subject further, because a dream is not just simply a dream, there are many aspects to it.

**Did you ever have a dream that came true? How would you feel if you had the ability to look into the future?**

(k) *The dream state – a state of altered consciousness*

### 3. Apparitions

There are different forms of apparitions and in this book I will focus on the three most common appearances: **Deathbed Apparition, Crisis Apparition** and **Apparition of the Dead**.
An apparition is a supernormal appearance that can be either a dead person, an animal or a living person. Many apparitions can appear real with definable form and features. They can look like humans and wear

clothing. In other cases, apparitions can be more of a fuzzy, luminous, transparent, hazy, and not well-defined form. Some people might see blobs of light, streaks, flashes or just patches.

*(l) It has been said that this photograph shows the ghost of Lord Combermere who was a British cavalry commander in the 1800s.*

*This picture was taken by Sybell Corbett in Combermere Abbey in Cheshire, England.*

**Deathbed Apparition:**

These are also referred to as deathbed visions and can be experienced by a person who is shortly about to pass away. Even people who were simply with a dying person have reported such phenomena. In most of these cases they spoke about the appearance of angelic beings, religious figures, dead loved ones or other luminous beings. The reason for this is often found in the close event of death and these apparitions come to support and guide the person who is about to transition. In Islam or Jewish tradition the figure of Azrael the Angel of Death is believed to help separate the soul from the body and assist in a smooth transition to the other side. (*Wikipedia 2020*)

**Did you ever have a near death experience? If so, what was it like? If not, do you know someone who did? What did they experience and how did this make you feel? If you were about to die tomorrow who would you like to meet and greet you on the other side?**

**Crisis Apparition:**

These forms of apparitions often appear if someone is going through an extreme crisis or particularly at the time of death. It has been said that the apparition appears to a loved one (who the dying person has close emotional ties with) to let them know that the person is just about to die or has just passed away. There are other phenomena in which apparitions appear as a sign of warning of danger. Especially common are such phenomena experienced by car drivers, who speak about seeing someone standing at the side of the road which made them slow down. Some belief systems say that the soul who had an accident at a certain place will stay there for a while to warn others and help them to not make the same mistake. I also believe that the term 'guardian angel' would fit in here perfectly. Whoever has gone through a really tough crisis and cried out for help will have come across the spontaneous helping hand that appears out of nowhere. Yes, I want to believe that you have.

**Have you ever reached out to a deceased loved one, when you felt helpless or hopeless? Did they respond – if not, are you willing to try?**

**Real Life Stories:**

This picture was taken by Sharon Boo in 1998, Fire Police/Photographer at Pawling (All Volunteer) Fire Department after a car crash. The woman survived the car crash, which was unbelievable for the firefighters and the police, she only had a slight arm injury. The ghost is believed to have been a guardian angel.

*m) Ghost appearance after fatal accident. Next picture I received by Elaine Johnson which clearly shows an Orb appearance at the middle top of the picture.*

Elaine said that this picture was taken in 2012 just a day after she received her diagnosis of breast cancer. She said she is sure that it was her dad trying to support her during those difficult times. Today, Elaine is clear of cancer.

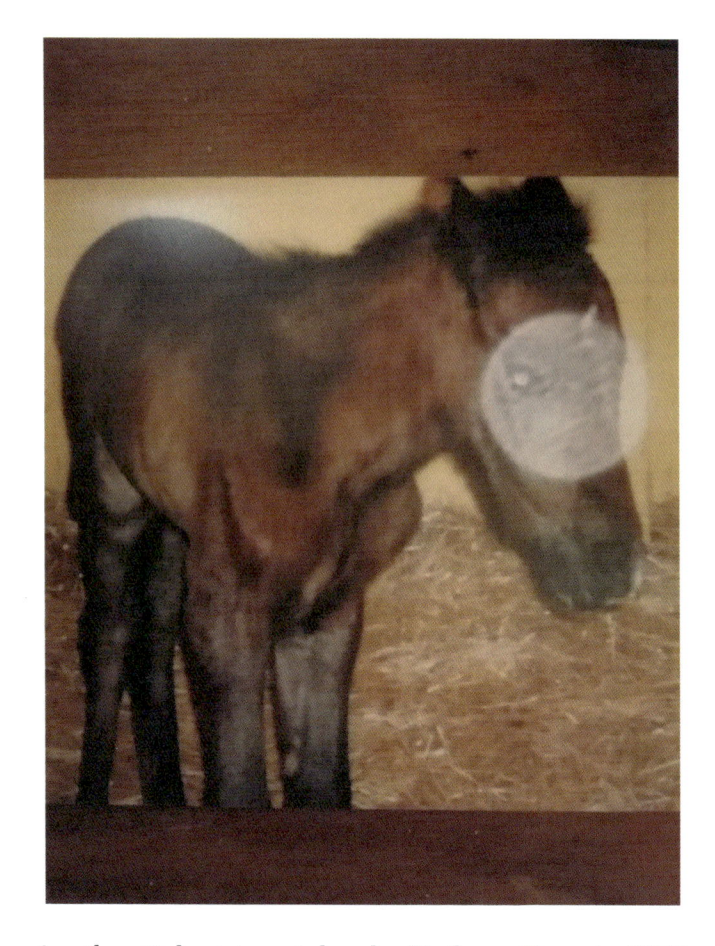

*Another Orb picture taken by Kathryn Shaw in 2008.*

This little baby lost his mother just a few days before this picture was taken. Does this show or prove that animals have a soul too?

**Apparition of the Dead:**

Again these apparitions happen mostly in times of crisis. Passed-over loved ones return to earth to communicate unfinished business, offer support and comfort to the grieving. Some of them are said to have given important information which was relevant for the loved ones who had strong emotional ties with the dead person. Also people who were emotionally tied to certain places have been said to return.

**My Real Life Story:**

I once saw an apparition and since then I am totally convinced that they are possible. It happened when I was on holiday for a few days. At that time, I was already living in England. A good friend offered her second home to me to recharge my batteries and spend some time in nature and away from the internet. I therefore did not have any internet connection or contact to anyone outside for a few days.

On the second day, when I woke up, I felt a pressure in my chest which didn't go away. At that time, I was already trained in psychic ability and mediumship communication and I felt that someone was around me and wanted to talk. I tried to push them away as I was on holiday and I didn't wanted to do anything spiritual. However, the more I tried, the more persistent the feeling was. So I decided to sit down for thirty minutes and write down everything that came through, to ease myself of the pressure. I had had great success with this many times before when a spirit wanted to communicate. I ended up writing a sort of letter or a poem and I felt quite sad when writing it. As if someone was about to say goodbye and was sorry. I even quoted one of Bob Marley's songs and in my letter I referred to a child that I left behind. Done and dusted, I put the letter aside and decided that in a few days' time I would ask my friend who owned the place if she knew anybody this might be relevant for. I also got some numbers and a name.

The next two days were alright and I had no pressure or any strange experiences. On the third day in the evening, when I had just relaxed in front of the fire, I suddenly felt really cold. The next thing I saw was a hazy, greyish silhouette standing in the door frame. I rubbed my eyes and it was still there. Suddenly it formed into a person and I could see features, and he wore boots like those for hill walking. Even though I was into spiritual things, I felt a bit nervous and ill at ease. I asked him a few questions but he didn't respond and just looked at me. Suddenly, he pointed at the hills and smiled. I asked him if he liked hill walking and he nodded. Still, I wanted him to leave and in this moment I didn't associate him with the letter I had written a few days before. I went upstairs to the toilet and there he was again. I thought maybe someone had died in the property and that I was now seeing them because I am really open.

I didn't sleep very well that night. I felt strange and nervous, awaiting the next day when I was able to tell my friend about what had happened. My friend didn't recognise anything in the letter I wrote, nor could she make sense of someone who had died in the property. I said to the spirit that I wouldn't go round now and ask everybody if they understood the letter or the apparition I had seen. People would think I was mad or crazy.

Once I got back home and turned my computer on, I went onto Facebook. Suddenly, I received a true shock. The first picture I saw was the guy looking exactly as in my apparition. The post stated that he was missing and asked if anybody might know where he was. Oh my God, that was truly shocking. I called my friend and told her all about it and said that I believe that he is dead and he has taken his own life. Now the letter made total sense as well. My friend said that she knew who that was and that her son went to school with his wife. I had to sit down and felt sad and helpless at the same time. I didn't dare contact his wife, what would I say? "Oh, I have seen your husband, he is dead and he actually hung himself and he feels very sorry → here is his letter." No, it was not my place to do that.

The next day another post popped up on Facebook, they had found him. He committed suicide through hanging himself. He was a musician and was very poetic too. He left behind his wife and a newborn baby. I was shocked and didn't understand why he would show himself to me. When I read where he had killed himself, I realized that two years ago I lived just a few miles away from the place where he took his own life. So I knew the area very well and a lot of times I went hill walking there too. I must have been the only person he was visible to because I was open and my friend's son went to school with his wife.

This was the only time I have seen a real apparition and it was certainly an experience, even though the circumstances saddened me and I was unfortunately not of better help to anybody.

**Have you ever seen an apparition? When? What did it look like? Were you scared? What did you do?**

**Some Rare Photographs of Spirit Photography** from the book *The Case for Spirit Photography* by Arthur Conan Doyle, first published by Hutchinson & Co. on 14 December 1922.

Spirit Photography is still a well discussed and controversial subject, however it is interesting to see what kind of pictures were taken back in the days.

Fig. 24.—Photograph of Mrs. R. Foulds, of Sheffield, with psychic photograph of her mother, obtained under good test conditions. Compare with Fig. 25. (See p. 125.)

Fig. 26.—Photograph of Mrs. A. E. Griere with psychic likeness of husband and father. The sitter was a total stranger to the Crewe Circle. Compare the lower face with Fig. 27. (See p. 127.)

## 4. Telepathy and Mind Reading

**Telepathy:**

Telepathy is a form of non-verbal communication over a distance.

Originally, this had to be done from a distance, then at a later date in 1963 they changed it so that the people involved can be in the same room and don't need to be miles apart for this to be able to happen. It is part of the classification of ESP in Parapsychology.

The typical experience is of the phone call you receive just after you have thought of someone. The mother's instinct we already spoke about would also fit into this category of phenomena.

Telepathy has been, and still is, a common investigation subject with different experiments that scientists and parapsychologists are interested in. Dr. Rhine, in particular, has done quite a few experiments in this field, and has tested mediums as well as normal people with regards to this ability.

After I read Eileen Garrett's Book, ***Adventures in the Supernormal,*** I was intrigued and keen to find out more for myself, so I asked the Parapsychologist and Paranormal Investigator Ross Richards from RBR Paranormal if he would be interested in assisting me with some experiments. Ross agreed immediately and soon we set up our own group to replicate Rhine's experiments.

"Telepathy, in its simplest definition and as I have experienced it, is direct knowledge of distant facts achieved by extra sensory means….The secret of telepathy sensitivity is very difficult to define. Even after years of observation of the processes involved, one cannot be certain that one has discovered all that means. Telepathy produces full and clear impressions in a way in which clairvoyance does not." (Eileen Garrett, *Adventures in the Supernormal, 1949*, p. 133)

*Pictures of Eileen Garrett kindly provided by her granddaughter*

## Zenner Card Experiment

The first experiment we did with Ross Richards from RBR Paranormal Investigations was the replica of Dr. Rhine's famous Zenner Cards test.

*(n) Zenner Cards*

I worked with the Zenner cards exactly as described in Rhine's experiments on ESP. I tried to guess the Symbols in an envelope and had difficulties in doing so. However, when Ross knew which was in the envelope it was much easier for me. Exactly as Eileen described in her book, I experienced the same issues.

In this experiment, again, he tested a lot of people and mediums and they had to read/guess a symbol that was hidden in an envelope. Dr. Rhine conducted this experiment to prove or find out about clairvoyance. A lot of people who thought they had good clairvoyant abilities failed in this experiment. For some parapsychologists, this showed clairvoyance didn't actually exist but was just happening by chance. However Eileen Garrett found a totally different explanation.

"I felt that Rhine's ESP cards lacked the energy stimulus which would enable me to see their symbols clairvoyantly. In fact, it would seem that the handling of the cards and their inanimate symbols inhibited, for the time being, whatever supernormal powers I possess. On the other hand, in working on clairvoyance tests with Dr. Rhine, I discovered that by being passed through the mind of another, the symbols came alive. My scores rose perceptibly. In the telepathy experiments, I was freed from direct concentration on the cards themselves and always able to receive the symbols from the mind of the transmitter, where they acquired vitality and provided the energy stimulus necessary for my perception." – (E.G. *Adventures in the Supernormal*, p.116)

Not quite satisfied with this idea, I wanted to test it out more and asked a group of students if they would be interested in taking part in the experiment.

I researched a lot into Dr. Rhine's experiments on telepathy and his findings. The more I read, the more I felt that I understood why some of them didn't work and how certain things could be tested differently.

## **The Telepathy Thought Transference Experiment**

We organized a group of people who were willing to take part in this experiment. The idea was to ask one of the students to transfer a symbol (which we showed her beforehand – Zenner Cards) to the mind of another student (the sitter). While the sender took an active state by sending the image mentally to the sitter, the sitter acted passively and was mentally open to receive. We found that if the sender was male, in our case they had more mental focus and willpower so the sending was more easily received by the sitter. If the sender was a woman, she had more problems focusing, doubted herself more and achieved fewer positive results with the sitter during the same experiment. I felt that this had to do with the focused energy of the mind which is often more developed in men than in women. Of course, women can have strong focused thoughts as well, but they tend to think more in emotions and are generally more complex.
## **Mind Reading Experiment**

The next experiment we did was about the ability to read another person's mind. We used the same symbols to keep the familiarity and hoped to gain more hits this way. For this reason, we asked one person to hold an image of a symbol before their inner eye. Another person now had to try to enter the sitter's mind and try to read what that symbol was.
There were those who had much more success in reading the other person's mind than they had with receiving or sending the symbol to the other person by will.

We also asked the sitter to give permission to the mind-reader and at other times we asked the sitter to consciously block the mind-reader from reading their mind. This way the reader discovered even more problems, just as we expected.

We also discovered that the people were much more confident with the telepathy, while when we asked them to do mind reading they were suddenly unsure if they would be able to do that. We thought the psychological pressure, their own inner voice and the thought of possible failure created an uncertainty that produces problems and leads to less success overall.

Clairvoyance differs from telepathy, mind reading or thought transference because it rarely happens under pressure. We don't expect to see an apparition and we can't force visions to come to us even though in some cases it can be induced or triggered. This works on a much subtler level and I feel that these phenomena need to be acknowledged as something different to telepathy. All of these phenomena involve mental images and the mind. A psychic reading includes the reading of the energy field or connecting with the soul of the sitter and not the reading of a person's mind, which again is a totally different process and doesn't happen under force.

**Different people will have different abilities, some find it easier to have a clairvoyance experience while others might find it easier to work with telepathy, mind-reading or thought transference. It depends on the person's personality, their brain structure, functioning or previous training as well as the stage of personal development.**

I immediately felt that Eileen was totally right and conducted this experiment with Ross from RBR Paranormal Investigations myself. I came to the following conclusion, similar to that which Eileen stated in her books:

1. Clairvoyance works with 'energy' from a living organism which cards are not made of.

2. The medium would be able to read the tester's mind, if the tester knew the answer (if the medium knew how to do mind reading).

3. The medium could do psychometry reading (reading energy from an object and giving information) but would then pick up on the energy of the creator of the cards or the person who put the card into the envelope because they touched it most recently.

4. The only way to see the symbol on the card in the envelope objectively would be through remote viewing.

## **Remote Viewing**

The phenomena of remote viewing is clairvoyance in space. It is the capacity to see scenes or events removed from the seer in space, and either too far distant for ordinary observation or concealed by intermediate objects. I am not sure if Eileen felt that telepathy is remote viewing because both have the objectivity at hand which clairvoyance doesn't have.

"The principal difference between clairvoyant and telepathic experiences lies in the relatively clear and simple nature of what one perceives telepathically. These pictures appear as things in themselves and are generally understandable as they appear. But in the clairvoyant experience, one follows a process….The lines and the pictures that they form do not always appear as clear representations of people, places and things, as in telepathy; rather, they are symbols whose meanings are not instantly clear to the sensitive as things in themselves. Nothing appears whole and finished that is "caught" is built up out of fragments and related to something else. It is necessary that the clairvoyant sensitive shall translate or interpret this information if they are to have any value for the person on whose behalf they have been sought, and this he does by means of that clear inner knowing which is also an element in the clairvoyant experience." (Eileen Garrett, *Adventures in the Supernormal p.130*)

*(o) Famous medium and founder of Parapsychology Foundation, Eileen Garrett*

I studied remote viewing and its phenomena and I came to the conclusion that it works differently to clairvoyance, mind reading, telepathy and thought transference. Which means that even a trained psychic or medium, mind reader etc. will not be able to do that easily if they follow the normal procedure. Remote viewing uses another part of the brain that is not accessed by other phenomena of second sight, I believe.

This is where these tests go wrong because the scientists or parapsychologists don't actually know how clairvoyance works. They think or expect it to be all the same, which it clearly is not. Only someone who has the actual ability or the experience can tell that the process is different.

Remote viewing is used by military and other institutions, especially in the USA. Russia and China. Furthermore, NASA used remote viewers to explore Mars before we were even able to fly there. Additionally, remote viewers are often employed by big companies in the USA to look for gold or oil in remote places.

I found that the ability to do remote viewing could be very helpful in tracking down missing people and might be used in psychic detective work.

I have taught remote viewing and its phenomena to students in Switzerland and Austria and both times the same experiences occurred. Those people were trained in clairvoyance and mediumship and in such cases this blocked their view. I tried to introduce new forms of exercise and the results they achieved then were great.

As you can see there are so many facets to this fascinating subject of clairvoyance. You might start somewhere and with training and development you discover abilities you didn't know you had.

## **Exercise 1 – Training your Clairvoyance:**

Over the years, I came across a lot of students who experienced all of the same problems when working clairvoyantly. The main problems were receiving clairvoyant pictures in the first place and secondly, how to make the correct interpretation of them.

I investigated the problem and I found that people who had problems with receiving pictures often lacked imagination. This lack could have been caused by social/cultural conditioning or a general block in their use of imagination and fantasy. Another reason is certainly true, the older we get, the more many of us lose our creative imagination because it is often not needed any more in our everyday lives. However, once we reawaken creative thought processes → clairvoyance becomes much easier.

Furthermore, the clairvoyant flow is blocked by having fixed ideas about what we should receive and scanning all the options of what it might mean.

**We need to learn to open our minds again – let's do it!**

**A) Take an object from your surroundings**, it can be anything. Let's say I will use a postcard that is hanging on my wall in my office.

**I place the card in front of me and ask myself the following questions:**

a) **Who** sent it?
b) **Why** did they send it?
c) **Where** from?
d) **When?**
e) **How?**
f) **What** is written on the card?

I take a piece of paper and a pen and write my answers down. Be creative. Make it up. Tell the story. Once you have answered all the questions, take another object. For example, a chair or a mug or whatever is in the room. Who made it? When? Who bought it and why?

Always go with the first answer you receive. Be creative, stupid, funny and just let it be a game that will help you to open your mind for clairvoyance.
Over time you will understand that the focus on one object can be the trigger that opens you up to totally different sets of stories and other pictures come to mind.

> **B) Exercise: Free Flow of Inner pictures**
>
> The first exercise helped you to learn how to trigger clairvoyance and create stories and widen your imagination. With focus and a sense of direction.
>
> Now, we want to relax the mind and allow any pictures to flow freely. This is often called creative visualisation. This time – no pressure.
>
> Choose a calm piece of music, allow yourself to lay down comfortably (if possible, wear an eye mask) listen to the music and allow any pictures to come up before the inner eye.
>
> Similar to daydreaming, but we use music to trigger our clairvoyant experience.
>
> You will feel how you become more and more relaxed and receive clairvoyant images effortlessly.

## 5. Ghosts and Spirits

This includes atmospheric psychic impressions, poltergeists and haunting phenomena.
Many people love the idea of ghosts and spirits and ghost hunting has become a very popular thing to do all over the world. The idea of exploring the unseen world and capturing evidence of their existence, with or without equipment, has always been very intriguing to many.
However, due to the high demand for paranormal experiences, the mass media has done its best to create false ideas of hauntings, poltergeists and other phenomena. This has led to a misconception of such phenomena. My intention in this book is to help to create a better understanding and to shed some light on the darkness.

**Have you ever had a paranormal occurrence? Maybe you have heard of haunted places. Have you ever visited one? How did it feel?**

**Ghost**

There is a difference between a ghost and a spirit, which many people don't know about. A ghost is classified as residual energy, an energetic imprint that is impressed onto a place, in space and time. It is not intelligent, it doesn't respond to communication and most psychics or sensitive people will be aware of such impressions by stepping into the field of the place or happening.

In this case your psychic vision gets triggered which will occur as pictures, feelings or even sounds or smells. It is more like the replaying of an old story. People can see scenes, experience physical sensations that can be daunting or scary and think there is a 'ghost' around them. In most cases this is not true and is often mistaken as such. In Parapsychology the term for such phenomena is apparitions or residual energy.

*(p) This picture shows an apparition of the Lady Townsend. Also known as "The brown lady in Raynham Hall", Norfolk in 1936. The story says that Lady Townshend was locked in a room to die after her husband found out about her infidelity. This event, for example, is very tragic and it is clearly possible that this lady Townsend still haunts these premises, unable to forgive the cruelty her husband has done to her. These phenomena could be referred to as earthbound spirits or an apparition of residual energy.*

*Photo: Wikipedia 2020*

## Spirit

A Spirit, however, is referred to as an intelligence that can actually respond to communications. A good example of this would be the "Hydesville Rappings," which mark the birth of modern Spiritualism.

A Spirit can be seen as an earthbound phenomenon which is tied to a place because of the tragedy of its passing, unfinished business or other emotionally strong connections. Unfortunately, it is often promoted that Spirits are bad beings similar to demons or the devil itself.

To understand the nature of these appearances of phenomena we just need to think about people in general. Once you leave your physical body you don't change much in your personality. Which means, if you have been a nice and loving person why should you suddenly be nasty and evil? Also, the belief that only bad spirits roam the earth is totally misunderstood in my eyes and just helps the ghost hunting industry to scare people further. A loving and devoted father or husband who suddenly died in a car accident can be tied to earth because of his bond with his family, wife and children. Grief can tie spirits to the earth and make them stay a little bit longer. I also truly believe that spirits too grieve their own passing and it is possible that the soul might need some more time to let go of the earthly ties.

**Have you ever tried to communicate with a spirit? What questions did you ask? Or what questions would you ask?**

## The Fox Sisters – The birth of modern Spiritualism

*(q) The Fox Sisters*

## The Hydesville Rappings

There is a beginning for everything. In terms of fringe science, the broadening of consciousness, most of the time, happens through a special event. By investigating individual limits, we experience a world that lies behind our own imagination and pushes to the borders of our own belief system. Nothing seems like it was before and the doors of perception are open to everyone who wants to enter them.
Anyone who has had such an experience knows about how hard it is to share it or explain it to others. Something like that must have happened to the Fox Family on 31st March 1848 when they became a part of a life-changing experience.

The Hydesville Rappings is one of the best-known paranormal events and marks the official Birth of Modern Spiritualism. In March 1848 civil war in Europe was on the rise and the interest in the Industrial Revolution had changed the life of many people on a material level. It seemed like the time was right for another Revolution, the Revolution of Consciousness.

On 31st March 1848, loud rappings disturbed the sleep of the Fox family. Unable to find any reason for the rappings, the Fox family did not know what to do, since the noise raised to such a peak. Then the daughters of the family seemed to have their fun by challenging the unseen noise maker with the clapping of their hands. They were all surprised, when the noise maker started to repeat their clapping. They asked for their ages, and they were given correctly. Aghast and surprised, the mother ran to the neighbours, because they were able to read and write. It was now easy to establish an alphabetical code and because of that it was possible to ask questions, which were also answered correctly.
With the help of this easy made code, they were able to identify the noise maker, who was a murdered pedlar that was killed by the former tenant, because of a dispute over money.

## The Truth Revealed

In 1904 the case was found to be true, when the remains of the pedlar and his tin box were found in the cellar of the house during some renovations. In the same year, it was published in a non-spiritual paper in the USA. A short while after that, all over the USA, circles were set up and a lot of people shared similar and different paranormal experiences.

The event of the Hydesville Rappings showed that no high education or technical equipment is necessary to speak to the so-called dead. The Fox Sisters were children, and they established an easy made code to make conversation with the spirit.

*(r) The Fox Sisters Home*

The case of the Hydesville Rappings also shows that there is (was) a higher intelligence behind those particular noises. The murdered pedlar was not making himself heard because he wanted to get justice. In fact, Charles B. Rosna was the pioneer of the spirit world who opened new doors of perception and built the bridge of intelligent communication between the bereaved (two worlds) and the so-called death.

However, not only simple people became interested in that kind of experience. Scientists from all over the USA started to do research into these happenings. As the case was found to be true, they deduced that there must be something more that humankind had not known about until this period in time.

It's not new to believe in a life after death, as in most of the ancient cultures there was a strong belief in that. But nowadays science has started to research in this area and the results are spectacular. While writing this book the Netflix Series "Surviving Death" has been released and holds very interesting insights into subjects of the supernormal and possible life after death. I can only recommend watching it and gain some interesting new insights.

By 1897, Spiritualism was said to have had more than 8 million followers all over the world. This was massive at that time and nearly unbelievable.

*(s) Frederic W.H. Myers*

### **Frederic W.H. Myers – Further Reading**

One of the curious scientists in 1900 was Frederic W.H. Myers, who formed the word "Cosmopathic" in his book, *Human Personality and its Survival of Bodily Death*. Cosmopathic means to be open to the access of supernormal knowledge or emotion. In the case of the Hydesville Rappings, it can be seen that children are more cosmopathic than adults. But adults can train themselves to be more cosmopathic and sensitive. The more you train, the easier is the communication with other spheres.

Further information can be found in:
Frederic W.H. Myers – *Human Personality* – 1903 –
ISBN 978148521408

# Mediumship, the Law and Brave Pioneers

It was not always easy for mediums to practice their gifts, even though many people believed in communication with spirits from beyond. In some cases, it was punishable by law. (You can read more below about witch hunts and trials.) A famous example of such legal prosecution is the case of Helen Duncan.

Victoria Helen McCrae Duncan (25 November 1897 – 6 December 1956) was a Scottish medium best known as the last person to be imprisoned under the Witchcraft Act of 1735. Her prosecution contributed to the repeal of the Witchcraft Act and was a major achievement and turning point for the 'legal right' for mediums to practice their craft/art.

If you want to read more about her story, search the internet for Helen Duncan and look for the disaster of 1941 with the sinking of the HMS Barham. You can also read her story in the book published by the Spiritualists' National Union – *The Two Worlds of Helen Duncan*.

*(t) Helen Duncan*

# Witch hunts and trials in the UK and America

Centuries ago, only priests were allowed to have visions and communicate with the divine. They understood themselves as the bridge between mankind and God and many misused their position of power. Back in those days, the poorer people in particular weren't able to read or write. This made it even easier for so-called priests to elevate themselves and spread their 'own' understanding of and self-interests in 'God's Message' to the masses.

Especially during the 16$^{th}$ century, people's superstition reached a new peak and the Catholic Church supported the idea that some people were practising witchcraft. This was of course totally the opposite of God's will and more often than not any unexpected ill-fortune, like the death of cattle, bad harvest, sudden death of a child or any other inexplicable happenings were said to have been caused by witchcraft.

It even went so far that the UK Parliament passed the Witchcraft Act in 1542. According to this Act, practising witchcraft was a crime and could be punishable by death. After five years, the Witchcraft Act was repealed but replaced by a new Act in 1562.

When James I came into power a new law was passed in 1604 which was focused on demonology. This led to the trials of the witches being moved from the churches to ordinary courts.

In 1542 over 40,000 people, mostly women, were killed. They were seen as devil worshippers, possessed by demons, or as practicers of magic. I don't even want to know how many world class mediums, healers, psychics, seers and astrologers, as well as holistic therapy practitioners, we lost through such accusations.

These witch hunts were not only in England and Scotland but all over Europe and America too:

"The Salem witch trials occurred in colonial Massachusetts between 1692 and 1693. More than 200 people were accused of practising witchcraft—the Devil's magic—and 20 were executed. Eventually, the colony admitted the trials were a mistake and compensated the families of those convicted. Since then, the story of the trials has become synonymous with

paranoia and injustice, and it continues to beguile the popular imagination more than 300 years later."
(Source - https://www.smithsonianmag.com/history/a-brief-history-of-the-salem-witch-trials-175162489)
Back in England, in 1736, the Parliament passed another Act repealing the law against witchcraft. This changed it from the death penalty to simply punishable by fines or the imprisonment of people who claimed to have magical powers.

While writing this book, I came across a major new cultural project to honour Scottish women persecuted as witches:

**Heal & Harrow**

"Women persecuted for witchcraft crimes in Scotland hundreds of years ago are set to be honoured in a major new cultural project being developed by two of Scotland's leading traditional musicians. A storytelling book, CD, podcast, visual art and a live touring live production are all planned to emerge under the banner of Heal & Harrow. The project - which will draw parallels with the treatment of women in modern-day society - has been directly inspired by a new campaign to secure a pardon, an apology and a new national monument for nearly 4000 Scots accused of witchcraft, the vast majority of them women." - *The Scotsman*, 12th Jan. 2021

## Getting to know your own story

This explains many of the deep-seated fears or wounds which a lot of us have of expressing our potential openly. For such a long time, people were imprisoned and killed if they claimed to have supernatural abilities. Psychic powers are latent in all of us and for some people they might appear as something magical or even supernatural.

When you start developing your own skills it can be the case that you experience times of despair or a fear of expressing yourself openly. The inheritance of past generations is still located in our DNA, as well as in the collective consciousness. It is really important that you acknowledge your hesitation and allow yourself to work through these memories very gently. Maybe you have been one of these witches or people in a past life and society has done horrible things to you. By staying aware and conscious you will be able to work through these memories and allow your full potential to come forward in time.

There are helpful things such as past-life regression, shamanic healing and others that can support you to remove these blocks from the past. By doing so, you also contribute to the whole of society, even humanity, and bring back what is very natural to us.

You may also go through a phase in your development where you will be confronted with people who challenge your practices and your beliefs. They might not take your development seriously or may even make jokes about you. It is important to stay very centred and not let this get to you. There are a lot of people who are not awake and who are still sleep-walking. Others might have also had bad experiences in the past and their ignorance now is helping them to cope with their own issues.

In my own personal development, I have experienced this quite a lot. Especially when I was younger, some people called me abnormal or even a witch. They probably didn't mean it in a bad way but more as a joke, but it definitely hurt me. I want to let you know that there are people out there who know exactly how you feel. People who have gone through exactly the same type of ignorance or painful awakening and they will come your way. Once you have decided who is on your side and supportive of your development so you can reach your full potential, things will change.

During your development you will also go through stages where you feel utterly alone and that no one understands you. Rest in this feeling and allow the transition to take place. It is very important that we spend some time on our own to acknowledge our innermost power and become aware of our own resources. You might lose a few friends along the way, but this is necessary so that you can make new friends who are more on your frequency.

I had no one to talk to about my abilities, nor anybody who understood how it felt to be me. It was only when I turned twenty-six that I met a person who actually knew what a Soul was. Just a year later, I found my way to Spiritualism and all of the pain that I had experienced in the past suddenly made perfect sense. Finally, I had people around me who totally 'got me', who knew what I was dealing with and furthermore I found community and friends who were supportive of my development. During my research on Spiritualism I came across famous people I admired who were active supporters of this movement and it made sense that I had always felt drawn to them.

## A Change of Fate – Mediumship becomes Legally Accepted

Luckily today Spiritualist Mediums are able to perform our work without needing to fear prosecution or ending up in jail. Thanks to the efforts of the Spiritualists' National Union (SNU).

"The Spiritualists' National Union (SNU) is a religious charity that supports Spiritualist Churches all across the United Kingdom, including the training of spiritualist healers, spiritualist mediums, public speakers and teachers."
(Source https://www.snu.org.uk/about-us)
"The Witchcraft Act, 1735 was repealed seven years later and was replaced by the Fraudulent Mediums Act, 1951, which many people believe was a direct result of Helen Duncan's conviction…..In April 2008, the Fraudulent Mediums Act, 1951 will be repealed and replaced by the Consumer Protection from Unfair Trading Regulations 2007 (CPRs) which implement the Unfair Commercial Practices Directive (UCPD)."
(Source - http://www.spiritualist.tv/news/mar08/helen-duncan.html)

It is important for me in this book to speak about the brave men and women who walked before us and prepared the path. Pioneers in their own rights, these people were inspired to find the truth and express themselves authentically. They argued that spirituality should no longer just be a privilege for the few and ensured that communication with other worlds was accessible to everyone.
I also remember those people who gave their life for their gifts, who lost everything just because they explored their own potential. In their honour, this book is dedicated to their work, their thoughts, their explorations and their knowledge. So we carry the torch of light and spread what is true everywhere.

How many of you were scared of your gift or are still worried about what would happen if you openly admitted what you are feeling, seeing or hearing?

A part of your psychic development challenge will be the overcoming of those obstacles, breaking through your own limitations and giving healing to those parts inside of you that have been neglected or buried. For those who believe in past lives, it can be helpful to clear the past away by exploring what happened in another life that might now be holding you back from acknowledging who you truly are.

# Learn more about
# Tracing your lineage in our Self-Study Course

## "UNLOCKING YOUR PSYCHIC POTENTIAL"

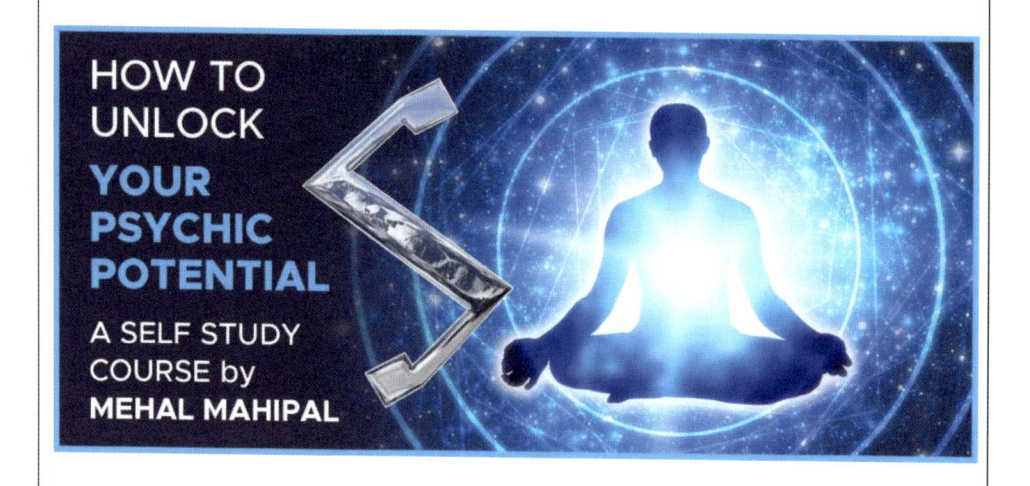

12 Video/Audio Lectures & Printable Transcripts
Proven methods & interactive assessments

**Bonus:** over **180 minutes** of Audio Meditations

**Learn at your own pace
with**

www.unlockingpsychicpotential.com

# Traditional Methods of Spirit Communication

## Table tipping:

"Table-turning (also known as table-tapping, table-tipping or table-tilting) is a type of séance in which participants sit around a table, place their hands on it, and wait for rotations. The table was purportedly made to serve as a means of communicating with the spirits; the alphabet would be slowly spoken aloud and the table would tilt at the appropriate letter, thus spelling out words and sentences. The process is similar to that of an Ouija board.

When the movement of Modern Spiritualism first reached Europe from America in the winter of 1852–1853, the most popular method of consulting the spirits was for several persons to sit round a table, with their hands resting on it, and wait for the table to move. If the experiment was successful the table would rotate with considerable rapidity, and would occasionally rise in the air, or perform other movements." (Wikipedia 2020)

(u) Table Tipping

**Ouija Board:**

"Talking boards often are controversial. Advocates feel the movement of the pointers are directed by discarnate beings or spirits of the dead. Sceptics say the user moves the platform subconsciously without realizing it. The best-known talking board is the Ouija Board, an oracle game invented in 1892 by an American, Elija J. Bond. The name is derived from the French and German words for "yes", oui and ja respectively.
Shortly after its invention, the Ouija enjoyed great popularity due to the interest in SPIRITUALISM and to the thousands of World War I bereaved who tried to find ways to communicate with their loved ones who had been killed in the war. Since then its popularity often has coincided with peaks of interest in the occult. Since 1966 the Quija has been marketed by the Parker Brothers game company of Beverly, Massachusetts, which states that it is a game for entertainment purpose."

- Source page 377, *The Encyclopaedia of Ghosts and Spirits* by Rosemary Ellen Guiley, Checkmark books, 2000

*(v) Modern Ouija Board*

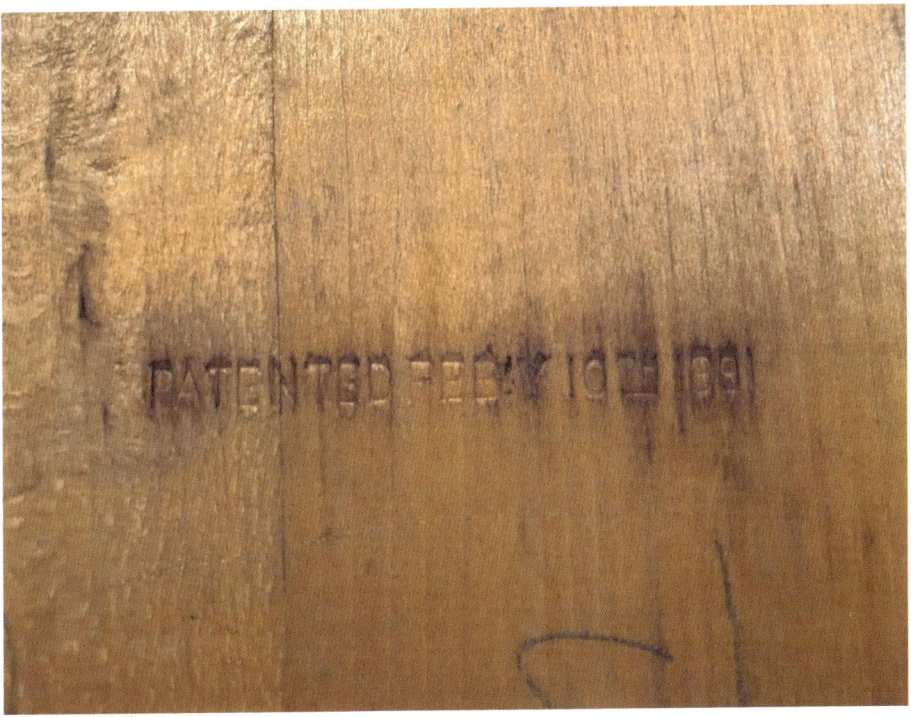

*(w) Two pictures of the original Ouija Board – patented in 1891*

**Spiritualist Seances:**

Seances became very popular, especially within the Spiritualist Movement. There were mental mediumship seances. In such seances the focus of spirit communication was mostly through the medium who acted as a channel for the spirit to speak or express themselves. There are many different forms of seances and in which form the spirit communication will take place depends on the medium themselves.

*An old picture from a séance back in the days. ( Source – Wikipedia 2020)*

A Seance is a kind of ritual conducted to communicate with a Spirit or Spirits. There are often different people present who don't know the medium at all. All of them long for evidence of survival after death and may hope to hear from their loved ones. Most of the time the people would gather around a table and at the beginning they would sing a hymn or song to put themselves in a state of harmony. It could also be seen as a modern way of invoking the spirits.

Physical mediumship seances were more focused on materialisations as evidence for life after death. This could have been that the medium's face changed, ectoplasm was produced, objects appeared out of nowhere, or furniture or objects started to move without anyone touching them.

Physical mediumship is very rarely performed these days and often the seances are by invitation only. In the olden days, people had to meet several times before they were allowed into a séance because it was said that the wrong people could disturb the harmony in the circle. So they had to make sure that the right people were coming together in order that the spirit would be more likely to communicate.

**Physical Mediumship:**

There have been some incredible physical mediums, such as the well-known Daniel Douglas Hume, who was even said to be able to levitate at one of his seances.

*The Levitation of Daniel Douglas Hume at Ward Cheney's house interpreted in a lithograph from Louise Figuier, Les Mystères de la science 1887.*

*Pictures: Wikipedia 2020*

Levitation might sound crazy at first, or nearly impossible, however I have heard of Buddhist monks who were able to do something like this. It requires years of training and knowing how to manipulate the magnetic and psychic forces. Even some scientists confirm that these forms of psychokinesis are possible and are doing wide research into levitation through sound and other means. My intent is not to convince you about something that you have not directly experienced, but rather to open your mind to the possibility that we have a much bigger potential than we might initially think. If you do your own research into this, I've no doubt you'll be surprised!

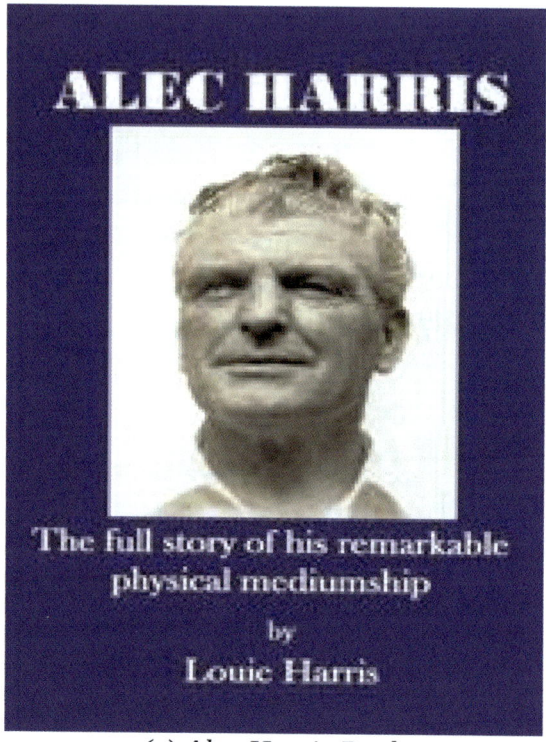

*(x) Alec Harris Book*

Another great physical medium who is worth mentioning is Alec Harris, a Welsh Spiritualist medium who was always sceptical about anything psychic till the day he had a life changing experience. There are several books on the market that are worth looking into. You can find some of them at the end of this book in the reference list for recommended further studies.

Seances took place all over the USA and the UK in the early 1900's and thousands of people attended them. However many of those so-called

seances were fake and genuine communication of spirit or production of phenomena were rare.
This doesn't mean they didn't exist, but they were not accessible for the masses.

## **The Spirit Cabinet Seances:**

Another tool that was often used for spirit phenomena or communication was the Spirit Cabinet.

The medium would take a seat in the cabinet, often tied up so that there was no fraud possible (which was important for many people who wanted to attend serious seances). The medium would hide behind a darkened curtain and enter into a higher state of consciousness in which a spirit would be able to manifest or speak through the medium.

The audience would sit in front of the cabinet and wait for the medium to appear or for psychic and physical phenomena to happen.
In modern times, we rarely find people working with the Spirit Cabinet and only a few know what it is good for and how to use it.
However I find a Spirit Cabinet very useful for personal spiritual development because it helps to contain your psychic energy more easily. The Spirit Cabinet can be used for Sitting in the Power, Trance Healing, Overshadowing (when the face of the medium changes) or Transfiguration (when a spirit takes over the medium and manifests its own form and face) as well as to produce of physical phenomena.

Originally, the Spirit Cabinet was invented by the Davenport Brothers (see the mention of their book in the reference list at the back) and here is a great article from RBR Paranormal Investigations that describes this in more detail:

*y) The Brothers Davenport & their Cabinet*

**The Spirit Cabinet**

The spirit cabinet is a very unique tool used as standard by many successful mediums over the years as far back as the mid 1800's when the spiritualist movement began to take hold.

**\*\*\* Cabinet Origins \*\*\***

It was invented by two brothers, Ira and William Davenport from America in the 1850's who toured the country performing shows of physical mediumship unseen before by the public. At one point they demonstrated in front of an audience of 1000 people.

They came upon the idea from an audience member to use some form of equipment to hold the energy of spirit so as to help in physical manifestation of spirit, and to make sure that no outside interference or fakery occurred during their shows.

They set to work on building such a contraption and soon had their spirit cabinet completed being seven feet high, six feet wide and two feet deep (see photos) though the dimensions were changed by other mediums to their own specifications. (see photos)

The idea of the cabinet was to section off the medium in the cabinet from sitters watching, both hand and feet were bound with rope so no foul play could occur, and seemingly impossible phenomena happened around them.

**\*\*\* Help From The Other Side \*\*\***

The Davenports were reported to have been in contact with the spirit of famous buccaneer Henry Morgan, who appeared to them during a show in 1850, became their spirit guide, and helped in communication with the spirit world.

Morgan was to be a part of their performances throughout the brothers' careers manifesting through voice and body. Other spirits communicated with them, and also used musical instruments the brothers had with them, as well as spirit hands appearing from nowhere.

### *** Famous People And The Cabinet ***

While some people thought of them as nothing but mere magicians and illusionists, a lot of people rallied around them, especially those in the spiritualist movement, notably one Arthur Conan Doyle, Author of the famous Sherlock Holmes, an avid follower of the spiritualist movement who believed that what they did was truly communication with the other side.

### *** Your Chance To Try The Cabinet ***

Since those times the Spirit Cabinet has been used throughout the world of spiritualism and physical mediumship to great success, which is why we at RBR Paranormal Investigations have decided to build one ourselves, together with Mehal Mahipal.

Though the cabinet we are building will be more compact and for one person to use at a time (see photos), it will be a great tool to work with alongside anybody, medium or otherwise, willing to have a go and see what we can discover.

We will also be using our specially designed Spirit Cabinet for overshadowing and transfiguration, with the sitter going into the cabinet, a light turned on above them with all other lights out, and a small audience to watch the sitter for any changes in the face or body to occur.

The changes can vary from one part, like the nose or eyes, to the full face changing which has been reported on many times in sittings of transfiguration.

*(1a) Ross Richard from RBR Paranormal Investigations, 2019*
*Our portable Spirit Cabinet which we use for Workshops and Experiments with RBR Paranormal Investigations. The red-light is an important tool when experimenting with overshadowing or transfiguration.*

*We have already used the Spirit Cabinet for several Workshops and public events. Here is a picture of Christine K. from Austria who came to visit one of our international workshops in the UK.*

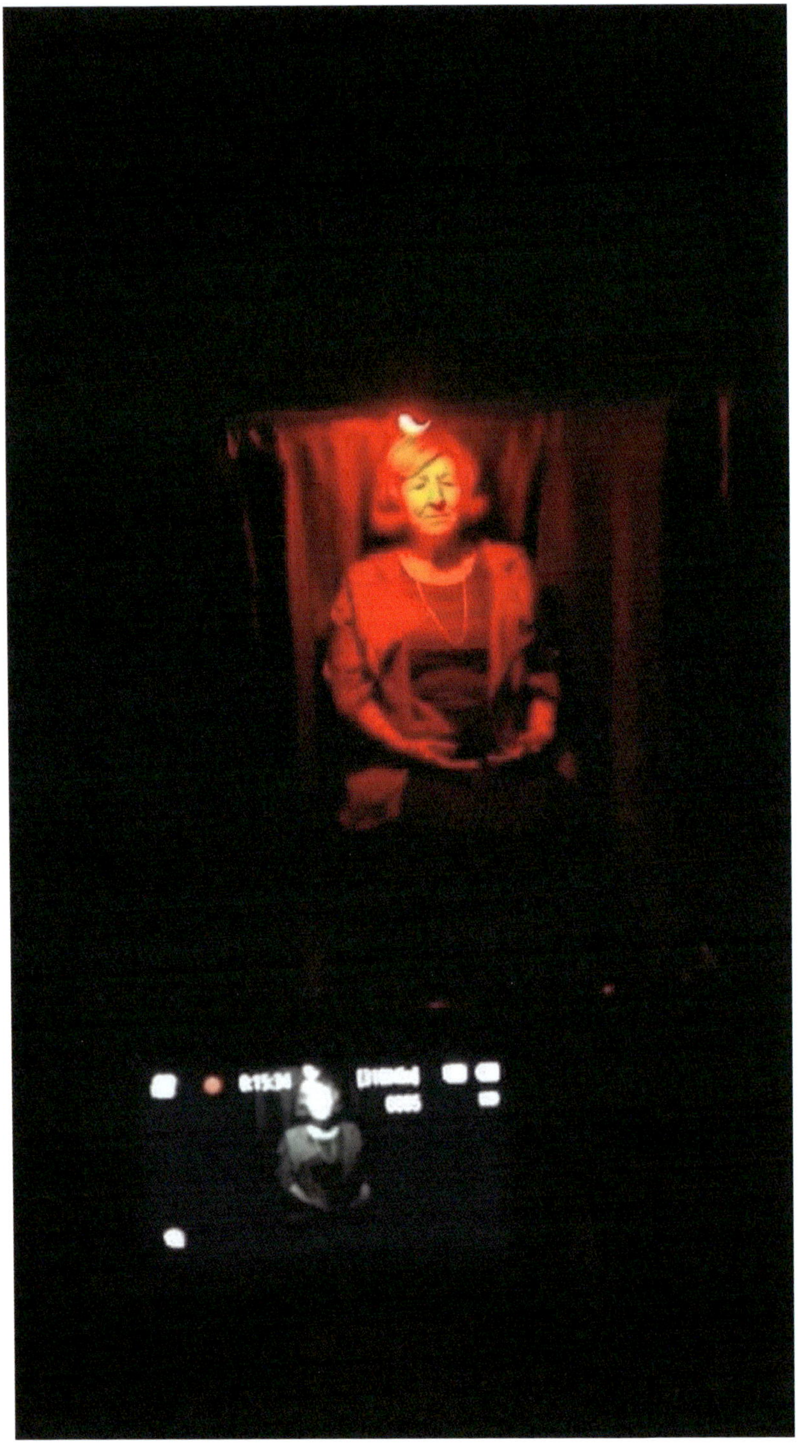

## Back in the days – Spirit Cabinet:

My great friend Elton Brumfield (also known as The Spirit Detective Historian/Psychical Researcher/Collector who locates Otherworldly Items of a Spiritualistic Nature) generously allowed me to publish one of his articles and original photo of an old Seance with a cabinet:

'This is an original photograph, (cabinet card), I own of the famous materializing medium, C. V. Miller, at a seance in San Francisco with Julia Schlesinger and other prominent Spiritualists. It was taken August 26, 1897 in Mrs. Schlesinger's home at a benefit seance for the well-known spiritualist newspaper, "Philosophical Journal". Mrs. Schlesinger edited her own California spiritualist newspaper, "The Carrier Dove" and was the author of a rare pictorial book of famous spiritualists titled, "Workers in the Vineyard". Yes, I have a copy of the book in my own little museum. This photo was never published in the "Philosophical Journal" and is probably the only one in existence, as I have never found it in any libraries or museums.

C. V. Miller was a materialization medium born in Nancy, France. He was living in San Francisco when Willie Reichel investigated him and described the results in a book titled Occult Experiences (London, c.1908). Miller's séances usually followed the same pattern: Miller himself would stand outside a cabinet, fully conscious (not in trance) and speaking throughout the proceedings. A variety of materialized figures would come out of the cabinet, frequently several at one time. As Reichel described it, "They came out one by one, spoke to the sitters and usually dematerialized in front of the cabinet. They sank through the floor." On one occasion Reichel's deceased nephew floated upward and disappeared through the ceiling. The most spirits Reichel saw at one time was twelve.

Miller visited Europe on two separate occasions. In 1906, he seemed to avoid contact with Lt.-Col. Eugene Rochas, the prominent French psychical researcher who had arranged for Miller to visit France. Instead, Miller held séances with Gabriel Delanne and Gaston Méry, Chief Editor of Libre Parole and Director of the Echo du Merveilleux. Méry said that he thought it probable that the phenomena produced by Miller were genuine, but "until there is fuller information we must be satisfied with not comprehending." The sitting was held in Méry's home, where Miller was stripped naked, examined by three doctors, and then dressed in some of Méry's own clothes. Miller was not allowed in the séance room prior to the sitting. Dr. Gérard Encausse (better known as the occultist "Papus"), stated in L'Initiation that his expectation was fully satisfied and that he believed Miller displayed mediumistic faculties more extraordinary than any he had encountered previously.

Miller went to Germany and gave well-received séances in Munich. Nandor Fodor stated, "The materialized form was often seen to develop from luminous globes and clouds which at first appeared near the ceiling. If several forms were materialized at the same time they were transparent." Although Miller stopped in France again on his way home to America, Professor Charles Richet reported that Miller would not subject himself to intensive investigation under the proposed conditions.

Two years later, Miller returned to Paris. On June 25, 1908, he appeared before forty people and gave a very successful séance under test conditions. The medium was stripped, examined, and dressed in black garments provided by the investigating committee, which again included Gaston Méry. The clothing had neither pockets nor lining. As usual, a number of spirits materialized and then later dissolved. Cesar de Vesme was unconvinced of the genuineness, though was unable to offer any explanations. Several others of the committee seemed doubtful. No more was heard of C. V. Miller after his return from France.'

## **Pendulum:**

"Pendulums can be made of different materials, some people using a simple necklace with a crystal or charm at the end. Be sure the bob or bobber – or weight on the end – is not too light or too heavy. It should weigh less than half an ounce. The best shape for the weight – or point – is something that comes to a point. The best length for the pendulum is six inches. You can make your pendulum or buy one.

The pendulum is a tool that is used to communicate with spirit via your higher self or your guides, and this tool can be used to aid you to make decisions about healing. It is a fast and easy way to get answers to problems, and one way that you can confidently make decisions based on a precise method. An interesting use of your pendulum is to find lost objects, and it can also be used to help you decide if a crystal is the right one for you to use." ( *by pendulumpsychics.com 2020)*

*(1b) Pendulum*

# Ancient Spirit Communication

If we go back in time and have a look at how ancient cultures communicated with Spirits we come to realize that it was only a select few who had the 'privilege' or possessed the 'powers' to do so. Those people were the shamans, medicine men and women, or the mediums of the old days. For years, they were trained to take on the role of communication between the worlds and in this way to bring healing, communication, blessings and insights to the community. Shamans can be found in any cultures and even today they still have a special role to play in the spirit connection between this and the other world. To become a shaman or shamanic practitioner is not an easy path and it takes many years of experience, practice, learning and understanding. Furthermore, it takes a lot of work on yourself. But for those who are brave enough to take the path of becoming a shamanic practitioner or who follow this calling, the harvest of the fruits will be many and they will have a lot to offer to others and to the world beyond.

*(1c) Female Shaman*

Shamans have different ways to connect with other realms and to communicate with spirit. Some of these methods are:

## Vision Quests:

A shaman withdraws into the wilderness, or at least somewhere in isolation for a few days. It is accompanied by fasting and often sleep deprivation. This leads to heightened states of consciousness and often gives them visions they normally would not gain.

## Fasting:

Reducing the amount of daily food intake results in heightened awareness and can lead to visions too. Also often used as a tool of cleansing body, mind and spirit.

## Dance:

Certain dances or movements can invoke not only change of perception but also attract spirits from other realms. In these states of ecstasy, shamans receive insights from other worlds and find answers to their questions.

## Drumming:

The monotone sound of a drum can lead to a certain trance state which allows the communication with other worlds more easily.

## Substances intake:

Shamans are well known for their knowledge of herbal medicine. For thousands of years, certain plants have been used to gain visions, insights and reach different states of consciousness. Those states were also said to be healing and purifying dependent on the herbs. The most common plants used for this are tobacco, marijuana, ayahuasca (mix of certain plants), psilocybin mushrooms or cactus, ceremonial cacao and others.

Most of the time the substances are used during ceremonial rituals and guided by people who know what they are doing. You shouldn't take any substances to alter your consciousness if you don't know what you are doing, and you should always consult an expert.

I don't encourage you to take any substances to reach higher consciousness as this can have a fatal impact on your personal life. There are many other ways in which you can attain the same results without using or taking any substances.

### Sleep deprivation:

Staying awake for long periods of time can lead to enhanced vision but also to hallucinations. Please consult an expert before trying this out yourself.

### Sleep State:

Many shamans receive messages in their dreams and hold holy communications with spirit while sleeping.

### Rituals/Ceremonies:

Certain rituals and ceremonies are held for the purpose of spirit communication. Often certain preparations are necessary for them to be successful.

**Have you ever done a Ritual? Did you feel how powerful they can be?**

# FREE GIFT

*Get Your*

## "UNLOCKING PSYCHIC POTENTIAL SACRED RITUAL"

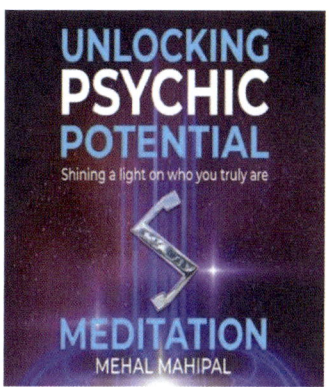

visit
*www.unlockingpsychicpotential.com*

to download it!

# Other Ancient Spirit Communications

## ANCIENT ROME & MYSTICISM:

The Romans were always very keen on signs and astrology, and used many of them in religious ceremonies. They worshipped the Gods and sacrifice was also a very important part of certain rituals.

The Romans took inspiration for their rituals from the Etruscans who initially were employed to perform rites and rituals. The Etruscans were members of an ancient Etruria in Italy, which is said to have been between the Tiber and Arno rivers. This urban civilization reached their peak in the 6$^{th}$ century BC. The priests who performed the rituals were called Augurs or Haruspex. An Augur was a priest and official in the classical Roman world. His main role was the practice of augury: Interpreting the will of the gods by studying the flight of birds – whether they were flying in groups or alone, what noises they made as they flew, direction of flight, and what kind of birds they were.

A Haruspex was a person trained in the art of divinity known as haruspicy. In such divinations, the person's job was the inspection of the entrails of sacrificed animals, especially the livers of sacrificed sheep and poultry.

Another example of the importance of divination and signs can be found in the early founding of Rome. Traditionally, the elder brother would have founded a new city but in the case of Romulus and Remus it was not clear who actually the elderly brother was. They were twins and at that time, with hardly any detailed records, it was not possible to tell. For this reason, it was decided that these two brothers would set out on a journey to the Palatine and Aventine hills.

This reminded me of the similarity of the Vision Quest, which is often a part of shamanic training, similar to a pilgrimage on which people set out to find answers for important questions. In the case of the two Roman brothers, it happened that one of the brothers, Remus, first happened to see a sign of six flying birds in a formation. While he explained to his brother what he saw, his brother Romulus suddenly became aware of twelve birds in a formation. Not able to decide if the number of six was good enough or the twelve which is two times six, the two brothers got into a bloody fight. While the two brothers were fighting, the legend tells that Remus jumped over a sacred furrow which had been dug by Romulus and he lost his life.

Whether this story is true or not, we don't know. All we know is that people have believed in a higher power, signs and symbols for a long time. Even to the extent that other people had to give their lives or lost their lives and it was seen as an omen or sign of the Gods. (Sources: Wikipedia 2020 and mariamilani.com)

*(1d) The interpretation of bird flight formations was a common practice in in Roman Empire*

# GREECE

## The Sibyls

The Sibyls were oracles or gifted seers in ancient Greece. The Sibyls prophesied at holy sites and their influence was from divine inspiration by a deity. The most famous one has been reported by Michelangelo on the Sistine Chapel ceiling in the Vatican.

The books of the Sibyls were highly worshipped by the Roman kings, especially Tarquin the Proud, who according to legend owned three of them. During times of crisis these books were consulted and guarded and kept by the Decemvirs. The books were kept in temples and guarded day and night like a national treasure.

## The Rise and Fall of the Oracle of Delphi

"Dating back to 1400 BC, the Oracle of Delphi was the most important shrine in all Greece, and in theory all Greeks respected its independency. Built around a sacred spring, Delphi was considered to be omphalos – the centre (literally) of the world.

People came from all over Greece and beyond to have their questions about the future answered by the Pythia, the priestess of Apollo. And her answers, usually cryptic, could determine the course of everything from when a farmer planted his seedlings, to when an empire declared war.

Arguments over the correct interpretation of an oracle were common, but the oracle was always happy to give another prophecy if more gold was provided. A good example is the famous incident before the Battle of Salamis when the Pythia first predicted doom and later predicted that a 'wooden wall' (interpreted by the Athenians to mean their ships) would save them.

The lack of a strict religious dogma associated with the worship of Greek gods also encouraged scholars to congregate at Delphi, and it became a focal point for intellectual enquiry, as well as an occasional meeting place where rivals could negotiate.

Delphi became a fantastic showcase of art treasures and all Greek states would send rich gifts to keep the Oracle on their side. It finally came to an end in the 4th century AD when a newly Christian Rome proscribed its prophesying."
(https://juanoracledelphi.blogspot.com/2011/10/history.html)

*(1e) Oracle of Delphi, Tholos*

## **Spiritual Principles**

### **The power of Prayer**

Over centuries, the power of prayer has been recognized and practised by millions of people in all religious cultures. Especially in times of crisis and desperation, it can be very helpful to surrender our worries to a higher power than ourselves. Filled with hope and positive expectations, people send out their loving thoughts to those in need. And yes, prayer does work – just like faith healing and anything else that you believe in. Faith is a powerful driving force that lets you overcome obstacles and limitations. It also offers protections and extra support when you need it. However, the belief in God has become somewhat out of date, especially in our modern society where technology and science seem to be the new gods on the block. We seem to slowly lose connection with our original roots, nature, the universe and furthermore our souls. Prayer can be a very helpful tool in times when we feel lost or alone, when we need help or just want to send some extra healing or help to others in need.
In fact, you don't need to believe in God as such, because even science can prove that mind over matter works. And those people who practice

the law of attraction know that when your vibration is right, you get what you have been asking for.

Prayer is still available to those who seek a more spiritual approach and would like to tap into the energy of millions who have been praying for centuries.

*1f) Prayer*

Others who would like a more modern or scientific approach could look into mind over matter, *The Science of Mind* and other works of Ernest Holmes. Who said that science can't go hand in hand with religion?

Ultimately, I understand prayer as something that can help you to elevate your vibration and direct your thoughts towards something higher. It is something that is good and worthy, something that brings joy and happiness, and only in this way will you change your life and the lives of others.

## Life is governed by laws and principles

"Earnest Shurtleff Holmes was the founder of the Church of Religious Science. Religious Science, like many New Thought faiths, emphasizes positive thinking, influence of circumstances through mental processes, recognition of a creative energy source and of natural law. Holmes had an immense influence on New Age beliefs, particularly his core philosophy that we create our own reality."

(Source - https://www.abebooks.co.uk/book-search/title/the-science-of-mind/author/dr-ernest-holmes/)

*(1g) Ernest Holmes*

A very powerful quote from Ernest Holmes from his book, *The Science of Mind,* puts the power of prayer into a new perspective:

"When people speak of prayer, they mean asking that some particular good come to them as a result of that prayer. We use a different word, one which more clearly defines the method by which we draw good to us. That word is 'prayer-treatment' or simply 'treatment'. We treat for results rather than pray for them in the old manner of pleading. A treatment is a definitive movement of mind, in a definite direction, to accomplish a definite purpose, There is nothing more real and effective than a treatment intelligently given."

# Clairaudience – Inner Hearing

**"My soul is a hidden orchestra;**
**I know not what instruments,**
**what fiddle strings and harps,**
**drums and tamboura I sound and clash inside myself.**
**All I hear is the symphony."**
- Fernando Pessoa -

Clairaudience refers to the ability of "inner hearing" or hearing with the etheric ear. A lot of people who are clairaudient are also clairvoyant or clairsentient too. Very rarely does this faculty appear all by itself. This refers to the ability of 'inner hearing' or hearing with the 'etheric ear'.

(1h) Music waves

Clairaudience is another common ESP ability and, during my years of experience in seeing other students developing their abilities, it often comes together with clairvoyance. Eileen Garrett states in her book, *Adventures In the Supernormal*, "It is impossible for me, except theoretically, to separate clairaudience from clairvoyance, for I have the clear impression of clairvoyance creating its own sound chamber; it is always accompanied by its own musical rhythm." *(E.G. Adventures In the Supernormal,* p.131*)*

Of course, this is how Eileen perceived her clairaudience. However, there have been people who were really clairaudient and not so much clairvoyant.

Inner hearing is best developed in stillness, which in our times seems to be a very rare occasion. Only then can we allow a bridge to be created between the physical and the etherical with no interruption. Clairaudience is the ability to receive words, songs, music and sounds on much finer frequencies with the inner ear. Therefore not 'audible' to others.

I found that the ability seemed to be more present in musicians, singers, public speakers, writers and in those who are strongly clairvoyant and clairsentient too. Artists who work with spoken language, words, sounds or music. I also believe that people who are really keen on music and listen to music regularly seem to have an enhanced ability of clear hearing.

However, clairaudience can be developed by everybody if we know how to do it. I will give you some exercises later in this chapter to help with this.

Throughout history, the phenomena of clairaudience has been present in different people. Those people who were known for hearing the voices of gods and spirits or who were able to gain inspiration from other realms mostly fell into these categories:

## Shamans:

They have many names and I refer to all the medicine men and women, the seers and healers who have been around since the beginning of time. (As discussed earlier.) Those who are able to create a sacred communion with the other worlds and receive insights, visions, and also perform rituals. These people often received their guidance through clairaudience and were told what to do to bring healing to others.

## Prophets:

Very well-known in religions such as Christianity, Islam, Judaism and other ancient religions such as Greek religion, Zoroastrianism, Manichaeism (Zoroastrianism or Mazdayasna) and others. Prophets have been said to speak the words of God, or to speak inspired by God. Often these prophets received their insights through clairaudience or visions and passed on messages to anyone who was ready to hear them.

A very well-known person was the sleeping prophet, Edgar Cayce. "Edgar Cayce (pronounced Kay-Cee, 1877-1945) has been called the 'sleeping prophet', the 'father of holistic medicine', and the most documented psychic of the 20th century. For more than 40 years of his adult life, Cayce gave psychic 'readings' to thousands of seekers while in an unconscious state, diagnosing illnesses and revealing lives lived in the past and prophecies yet to come."
(Source - https://www.edgarcayce.org/edgar-cayce/his-life/)

**Channellers:**

Channellers are able to perceive visions, sounds, words of wisdom, future potential, philosophical thoughts or healing. The most well-known form in this modern time, for receiving insights from the divine or other worlds, is a person who channels messages. Normally, the person would enter into a Trance State and would then channel words of wisdom, healing or inspiration. The words can be of high quality and bring real change to the listener, but this will depend on the medium's personal stage of development. The channelled messages can come from their own subconscious mind, the higher self, spirits, entities or other worlds.

Highly-trained Trance Mediums allow spirits to take possession of them and let the spirit use the medium's voice box to act as the catalyst for speaking. In such sessions, the medium clearly changes and the voice can take on the voice of the deceased. This phenomenon is not seen as pure clairaudience but rather is classified as Trance Speaking. Some Trance Mediums put their channelled messages in the form of paintings. Moreover, some of those people were unable to paint at all before they went into a Trance State.

*(1i) Channelled Picture by Sharon Shaw*

### **Artists:**

Can use clairaudience to receive 'inspiration'. Especially artists who work with words, sounds, music, singing etc. Visual artists might receive inner pictures of what they should paint. This inspiration often comes from a higher source outside of themselves.

### **Healers:**

Might use clairaudient ability to find out about a client's health issue or what type of healing should take place. See the abilities of Edgar Cayce:

"Later in life, Cayce would find that he had the ability to put himself into a sleep-like state by lying down on a couch, closing his eyes, and folding his hands over his stomach. In this state of relaxation and meditation, he was able to place his mind in contact with all time and space – the universal consciousness, also known as the super-conscious mind. From there, he could respond to questions as broad as, "What are the secrets of the universe?" and "What is my purpose in life?" to those as specific as,

"What can I do to help my arthritis?" and "How were the pyramids of Egypt built?" His responses to these questions came to be called "readings," and their insights offer practical help and advice to individuals even today. Many people are surprised to learn that Edgar Cayce was a devoted churchgoer and Sunday school teacher. At a young age, Cayce vowed to read the Bible for every year of his life, and at the time of his death in 1945, he had accomplished this task. Perhaps the readings said it best, when asked how to become psychic, Cayce's advice was to become more spiritual." ( Source - *www.edgarcayce.org/edgar-cayce/his-life/*)

## Crisis:

There are recordings of people who heard a voice of warning before something bad happened. Some people believe that this was their guardian angel or God speaking to them. Others refer to this phenomenon maybe as intuition or a higher self who can send messages of warning.

## Recovery:

In ancient Greece, there were temples in which people could go when they were ill and where they practised healing sleep. These temples were called Sleep Temples. Many recordings have been passed down, in which people spoke about extrasensory perception during their sleep. They had seen a luminous being of light and heard voices speaking to them saying they would get well soon. Maybe you have had such an experience yourself, a dream in which you encountered a voice or a being telling that told you would get better soon? It is also possible to receive such impressions about other people close to us.

## Greek Sleeping Temples:

"Sleep temples (also known as dream temples or Egyptian sleep temples) are regarded by some as an early instance of hypnosis over 4000 years ago, under the influence of Imhotep.

Sleep temples were hospitals of sorts, healing a variety of ailments, perhaps many of them psychological in nature. The treatment involved chanting, placing the patient into a trance-like or hypnotic state, and analysing their dreams in order to determine treatment. Meditation, fasting, baths, and sacrifices to the patron deity or other spirits were often involved as well.

Sleep temples also existed in the Middle East and Ancient Greece. In Greece, they were built in honour of Asclepios, the Greek god of medicine and were called Asclepeions. The Greek treatment was referred to as incubation and focused on prayers to Asclepios for healing." (*Wikipedia 2020*)

*(1j) Temple of Asclepius in Greece (Wikipedia 2020)*

*1k) Asclepios giving healing whilst people sleeping in temple, Wikipedia 2020*

**Near Death Experience:**

Another very common form of clairaudient impression happens with Near-Death Experiences. Many people who have been on the threshold of life and death have returned and said they have seen a light, a tunnel or other forms of loved ones and beings. Eighty percent of those people refer to clear communication with those beings or say they heard a voice which did send them back to earth. Others referred to voices who brought comfort and reassurance that everything would be okay.

**Spiritualist Medium:**

In Spiritualism the ability to perceive sounds, words, voices etc. clairaudiently is often found in Spiritualist Mediums who give evidence for survival after death. They often mention that they heard a word that triggered other pictures inside of their mind which led them to 'tell a story' about the loved one.
Information can be received differently and it all depends on your own ability. Some mediums may hear a siren and it indicates for them the loved one died in hospital. Other mediums would receive a picture of a

hospital clairvoyantly to get the same message. I have also come across mediums saying that they could hear a certain song and used this information for evidence of the loved one to the sitter.

A sound or word can act as a trigger that will help to give the right interpretation for the pictures you might see. Some mediums say they actually hear the voice of the passed over spirit and he/she is telling them what to say.

Later in this book, I will dive deeper into this process and the work of a Spiritualist Medium.

I know that clairaudience can be a powerful psychic ability in many different areas. My clairaudience is quite developed and I have had many different experiences from hearing inspiration, music, sounds, words and voices. Everybody is different and their psychic ability expresses itself in different ways.
Sometimes it comes naturally over the course of time and can never be forced. It is important to stay open and see what happens.

---

**Super Tip!!!**

1. When you sit to develop your psychic abilities, especially clairaudience, I would recommend you wear an eye-mask and ear plugs – this allows you to sit undisturbed.

2. Focus on developing one sense at a time. Especially when you are a beginner. Give yourself a week or two, or longer –whatever suits you – and just work on that one ability. This will help you later on to deepen your practice and experience.

3. Learn to listen to music actively. When you feel your mind wandering off bring it back to the music. If you get impressions or pictures in your mind – bring it back to the music. It takes a bit of concentration to focus and develop clairaudience in this way but it will pay off eventually.

If you focus on developing one sense, then other senses will also automatically follow to enhance it.

# Clairsentience

*"I believe in intuitions and inspirations…
I sometimes FEEL that I am right.
I do not KNOW that I am."*
- Albert Einstein -

This is the most powerful of all the clair senses, because it helps you to interpret the impressions which you have received.

The basic ability of clairsentience is latent in everybody and often understood as the language of the soul, or your intuition. In its advanced and highly developed form, it can reach an exceptional level of clear knowing.

The basic form of clairsentience responds to the navel chakra, where our gut is located. Here we have access to our intuitive feelings and understanding. The place in which we immediately feel that something is wrong or doesn't 'feel right'. Remember when I spoke about the intuitive state? Yes, this is where it is. Many people are aware of feelings, of what is right or wrong, but it doesn't go beyond that.

The next level of clairsentience is when it comes to the true catalyst to release energy.

This means you would enter into the state of an Awakened Intuitive and act upon your intuition. No doubts, no regrets, but knowing what is right. This trust in our own psychic force or power creates confidence. In this way, the solar plexus chakra will be activated. Suddenly understanding becomes a personal driving force that seeks to express itself authentically. It's your inner compass, your guiding light.

It is something that can clearly guide us without words and often we rely only on what we feel. Acting upon that without thinking where it may lead you. This takes courage. Many people who experience blockages in their psychic development have either a blocked or weakened solar plexus chakra. Such people have experienced loss of power or suppressing in the past. This is why they have problems in expressing how they feel and are denying their own truth Due to this, they don't follow up on an intuitive feeling because the energy is blocked and can't flow freely. Only when the solar plexus is used as a catalyst and becomes an energetic driving force do we suddenly gain more confidence in our abilities.

It's a big step to move from the Intuitive to the Awakened Intuitive state. It will require self-discipline, to restore personal power and get in touch with your real feelings.

This means that we need to work on our personal development, not only on the clair senses. To transform your clairsentience to the next level you will need to uncover suppressed and hidden aspects inside of you. It will require you to bring up, deal with, and undo any restrictions that have been put upon you. This starts with diving deep into the wounds of 'when we weren't allowed' to be ourselves. Undoing the social conditioning of when we are told who we should be. Forgiving others who hurt us and retrieving our soul parts and energy from people and situations that made us feel small, unworthy, or abused.
If you take this step, your clairsentience will change. It will turn into clear knowing, without the doubts, the fears and the uncertainty.

This means that we need to learn to become brave, confident and authentic. To truly let our light shine bright, we should let go of our inner critic, thus healing this trauma and uncovering our true greatness.
For this reason, the development of your psychic potential is a path of self-discovery.
Your true 'psychic' potential lies hidden under all of the lies others told you, and which you believed because you didn't know better.
The more you work on yourself and overcome inner and outer obstacles, the more you will see clearly who you really are. Training your psychic abilities is so much more than doing exercise after exercise in a course. It's more about transforming the self. Furthermore, it is learning who you can really become.
On my own path, I was lucky enough to have met teachers from all over the world who understood the importance of self-development and self-healing. In this way I was able to discover parts of myself that I had never known even existed.

## **Buddhism – Clairsentience and the Heart Space**

I once went on a Buddhist meditation retreat down South in Devon. On this retreat, each day different teachers came around to teach. We were encouraged to ask any questions we had or share our thoughts. We all sat in a circle around the teacher and suddenly no one dared to speak. I felt that people were too shy to ask a "silly" question and no one wanted to sound stupid. Because no one spoke, I took the chance and asked something about a specific meditation practice I struggled with. By doing this, I thought I might inspire others to speak too, but the others stayed silent.  Suddenly the teacher looked at one of the students and said: "I know what your question is….!" and the teacher quoted exactly the question that was on the student's mind. The teacher continued to do so with a few other students and everyone was blown away by how he could so accurately read our minds.

"How did you do that? I mean how can you know what other people think?" One student wanted to know.

"I just know," said the teacher and smiled, "it's in here," and he pointed his finger to his heart.

Even I was impressed by the accuracy the teacher showed regarding knowing what the students wanted to ask. I have only seen this with a few very highly developed mediums before. In this moment, it occurred to me that the answer must lie in the heart space. I started to research deeply into chakras and the connection with the development of psychic senses. It confirmed exactly what I had assumed in the first place. There are different levels of intuition and the highest level is clear knowing without any doubt, it only appears in people with well-developed heart chakras.

People have to be trained differently when it comes to the clair senses. I truly believe we should consider the importance of the chakras and their meanings when training in psychic development. Once someone has developed strong intuition, they need to make sure the solar plexus chakra is working properly and once that is done, we can then move on to the heart chakra. This is why personal development is so important in discovering your psychic potential and also works the other way around.

Additionally, I found that once the heart space is fully developed it allows you to also use much less energy for your psychic work. However only, but only, if all the other chakras are working properly too.

Clairsentience will help you to truly gain the ability to interpret any psychic impressions, no matter if they are received clairvoyantly, clairaudiently, clairgustantly or via psychometry.

For me, this marked a real high point in the realisation of psychic potential.

Slowly but steadily to soften the heart and open the heart space. Definitely not an easy task, but worth it – the opening of the heart space will transform your life.

I have created a quick exercise for you to try out at home. This way you can start working on these two levels and learn to improve your clairsentient ability.

## 1. Exercise:

a) Make a list of all the things you always wanted to do but didn't have the courage to do yet. Anything that comes to mind, don't censor yourself and don't limit yourself either.

b) Now make a list of all the things you are scared or fearful of. Again, anything that comes to your mind, no matter how long or short the list may be.

c) Take the first list a) and use another piece of paper to write all the single points down so you can cut them out individually. Cut them out. Fold each of the words/things up into small bits so they have the same size and you can't tell which is which. Shuffle all of them in your hand, then throw them on the floor and pick up one. Open it and see what it is.
→ Now find a way to make it happen!!!!

PS: If you had thought of something that sounds impossible than imagine it with every fibre of your being and see yourself doing it.
Trust me, it really works. In my shamanic work I do this all the time. This helps you to overcome limitations of the mind, space and time. And this is what you do when you work with psychic energy, isn't it?

d) Take the other list, do exactly the same. Write all the points on another piece of paper and cut them out. Fold them so you can't tell which is which. Shuffle them, throw them on the floor or table and pick one.
Here we go → Challenge accepted? Find ways to confront your fear.
It's not about how long it takes. It's not about force – it's about not limiting yourself and finding ways to overcome this inner obstacle. The voice that is telling you that you can't do this.
This will help to open up and strengthen your solar plexus chakra – overcome fear.

PS: And don't forget to let me know how you got on, what you did and how it felt for you. I love hearing from you. You can email me on info@mehalmahipal.com

> **Exercise 2:**
>
> Healing the Heart Space – A Buddhist Practice
>
> We hold a lot of energy in our heart space. Much of it is trapped energy, painful memories, fear of being rejected, abandoned or not wanted. A lot of these memories can lead to a blockage of the heart chakra and don't allow you to live to your full potential. I want to show you a technique that is both incredibly powerful and easy to follow at the same time.
> It will help you to cultivate love and compassion, firstly for yourself and then for others. Slowly, you will feel how your heart space relaxes, opens up and slowly releases all of this trapped energy. In the long term your clear knowing ability will get stronger and increase.

## **Buddhist Love and Kindness Meditation**

### **1. Metta for the self – 5 minutes:**

(Feelings of peace, calm, tranquillity → grow into feelings of strength and confidence, then develop love in your heart.)

Focus on your breathing and allow this mantra to deeply penetrate into your heart space.

MAY I BE BLESSED
MAY I BE LOVED
MAY I BE HAPPY
MAY I BE SAFE

Repeat Mantra

Observe how you feel and what happens in your body.
Tingly feeling? Tension? Warmth?
Don't judge whatever happens or if you find it difficult, keep going, surrender
→ There might a point where you feel that you want to stop → stillness prevails

→ if your mind starts thinking → Repeat the mantra again and observe the energy in your body.
It's a time to give yourself blessings and increase the feeling of self-love

## 2. Metta for a friend – 5 minutes:

Think of a good friend. Bring them to mind as vividly as possible, think of their good qualities.
Feel connection with your friend, your liking for them, encourage feelings to grow and repeat the Mantra.

MAY YOU BE BLESSED
MAY YOU BE LOVED
MAY YOU BE HAPPY
MAY YOU BE SAFE

Shining a light from your heart into theirs.

## 3. Metta for someone you are neutral towards – 5 minutes:

Think of someone you don't particular like or dislike. Neutral feelings. Someone around you. Reflect on their humanity – include them into your Metta.

MAY YOU BE BLESSED
MAY YOU BE LOVED
MAY YOU BE HAPPY
MAY YOU BE SAFE


## 4. Metta for someone you dislike – 5 minutes:

Think of someone who you actually don't like, an enemy or someone you have difficulties with. Don't get caught up in feelings of hate, think of them positively and send them Metta.

MAY YOU BE BLESSED
MAY YOU BE LOVED
MAY YOU BE HAPPY
MAY YOU BE SAFE

## 5. Metta for the world – 5 minutes:

In this final stage after you have sent Metta to yourself, for your friend, a neutral person and someone you don't like, now you are asked to extend these feelings further. Extend those feelings to everyone around you, everyone in your neighbourhood, town, country, the world.
To all beings elsewhere.

MAY YOU BE BLESSED
MAY YOU BE LOVED
MAY YOU BE HAPPY
MAY YOU BE SAFE

Gradually relax out of the meditation and bring the practice to an end.

---

### Free Gift

### *Get this Buddhist Metta Meditation Session:*

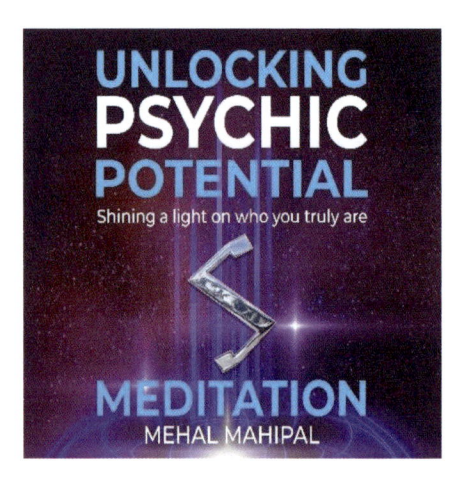

*By visiting www.unlockingpsychicpotential.com to download!*

# **Clairgustance**

*"You have your way. I have my way. As for the right way, the correct way, and the only way, it does not exist."*
*- Friedrich Wilhelm Nietzsche -*

This is another rare psychic ability and not really common in many mediums. I believe that has to do with being so closely connected to the physical ability for tasting. It is difficult to distinguish between the etheric counterpart and the physical.

I once came across a person who had a very heightened sense of taste and it was certainly more developed than in the average person. Again, this person was not spiritual at all and was not aware of psychic abilities and their purpose. I met him about fifteen years ago at a friend's house. All of us wanted to order some take away food and when we were about to put the order in, he said that he couldn't eat take away food. First, I found it quite funny because he seemed to be a bit of an eccentric person anyway, till I discovered the true reason. He told me that he was unable to eat any food that was not prepared by himself.

When I asked him how this came about, he told me about his heightened sense of taste. "If I eat food which is made by other people, I just can't eat it because it makes me sick right away. They use too many or too few herbs and spices, sometimes it's the wrong combination of spices and it's absolutely awful. It just tastes so wrong."

I was intrigued to know more and find out if that was maybe just a sign of a psychological problem. "So when you cook for yourself, how do you know then how much you need to put into the meal and which herbs match together?"

He looked at me, "Well, it might sound crazy, but when I cook I can see colours in front of me. When I pick up a herb or a spice the colour changes and if they match together I just know because the colours are in harmony."

This was rather interesting as I had never come across such a person before.

"I am not fussy, I just can't help it. I have always been like that since I was a child. And I love food but it needs to be done correctly!"

His friend confirmed that he was an exceptional cook and whenever he cooked a meal it tasted amazing. They also told me that he had a twin sister but she didn't have this kind of 'problem'.

A rather interesting encounter and again I was aware of how heightened senses could express themselves in many different ways.

Let's do some short exercises to train our taste buds and dive deeper into this subject.

> **Exercise:**
>
> I invite you to try to taste different vegetables, fruit, nuts, spices, herbs etc. and see how your body reacts to them. Do you see any colours? Do you feel any different?
>
> Also pay more attention to detail when you cook and let your intuition guide which ingredients you want to use.
>
> The more you train yourself in this area, the more you might well develop an etheric sense and it will trigger feelings and pictures that will help you in your development.
> To engage with food and taste is a great physical pleasure and can at least enhance your quality of life in this physical incarnation.

## Clairtangency (clear touch) – Psychometry

*"Touch has a memory"*
- John Keats -

Psychometry is the ability to read energy from an object. Every object holds an energetic imprint from who made it, to the person who owns it now. It also holds information about the locations where it is/was kept, as well as allowing it to create an energetic rapport with its owner.
Psychometry is a known tool in Psychic Development and allows us to explore new ways of learning about energy. It can be used by Psychic Mediums, who can give Readings for the owner of the object. Or it can be used as a trigger to connect with the sitter. Additionally, it is a good tool to use less of your own psychic energy when connecting with the sitter.

This is a very common tool that is used by Psychic Mediums or Psychic Detectives but not so much by Spiritualist Mediums who bring evidence for life after death.

**Psychic Detectives** can use Psychometry to build an energetic link with a missing person and more easily blend with their energies. This way it is easier to trace back the last actions or trails of the person and hopefully find them more quickly. Not all psychic detectives use psychometry in their work.

**Spiritualist Mediums** can use an object of a passed-over loved one to build a link to the spiritual realms and the soul of the sitter.

## Clairscent – Clear Smelling

**"You're only here for a short visit. Don't hurry, don't worry. And be sure to smell the flowers along the way."**
**-Walter Hagen-**

Over many years, I have seen quite a few mediums working now and again who gave clairscent evidence during one of their public demonstrations. The most common statements I heard related to their clairscent were 'tobacco' or 'perfume' which they said was associated with a deceased loved one.

In both cases, it was evidence for a personality trait of the deceased and helped to find the right sitter in the audience. Furthermore, it also acted as a trigger for the medium to get more clairvoyant pictures.
Such phenomena can appear in paranormal investigations – it has mostly been reported that the smell of mould or of something 'gone off' was experienced.

I discussed this subject with a few colleagues of mine and we all agreed that clairscent is a rare, unreliable, and open-to-error encounter. It is so close to the physical experience that we often can't tell if the smell is actually in the room or if it's perceived via the clair senses.

## **Real life Story – Yogesh Kumar – Das Parfum (Vienna)**

I came across a very interesting experience regarding the phenomenon of clairscent when I was teaching Psychic Abilities in Austria in 2018. I found a business card in the venue where I was teaching, which was from someone who makes individual perfumes. Something inside of me was really intrigued, so I went onto his website to get more information. Yogesh Kumar is a rare phenomenon of a 'real' clairsentient and creates individual perfumes inspired by the person's 'body' smell.
I had never heard of something like this before and found it rather fascinating. For this reason I contacted him and asked if I could come around and hold an interview with him about his work. Two days later, my friend and fellow medium Anita Ratschiner and I sat in his little shop in Vienna. Yogesh Kumar was very open about all the questions I had and his story was truly a magical encounter that I had never come across before.

He was born in New Delhi to a lower-middle-class family. From an early age, he realized that he had a gift that others seemed not to have. He could smell if there was tension in the air or if something was about to happen. This confirmed with me what I had felt in the first place, he was actually gifted with inborn psychic abilities. His heightened sense of smell led him to create his very own first light, spicy, woody blended Eau de Toilette as a birthday present for a friend at the age of thirteen.

From the age of fifteen, Yogesh travelled widely. On his journeys, he started exploring his gift of clair smelling. He soon realized that he only wanted to follow his passion and needed an audience who valued this awareness as an art in itself. On his search to find himself and to find love, he landed in Vienna in 1997. Yogesh perceived that introspection was a missing quality in the people and he wanted to change that.

In his work, Yogesh combines his insights about the client's consciousness combined with the impact a fragrance has on a person's limbic system. Soon, he realized that there was potential to create a business out of his unique gift and started offering his individual perfumes to a wider audience.

When I asked him how he would decide on the right fragrances, he said, "I use a scarf that you have worn and smell it. Alternatively, if I may smell on your neck, this allows me to explain the elements (Ayurvedic concept) and the character of your body."

Yogesh's process of consultancy: "I use the strength and the weakness of your personality according to the Ayurvedic concept (The Ayurveda Fragrance Terminology methodology is unique in the world. It makes it possible to combine Ayurvedic principles, thousands of years old, with the latest findings in olfactory research). This fundamentally distinguishes our offer from all other products in the scent marketing area."

The principle:
"The practice of AFT consists not only of normal laboratory work, but also constitutes a world view in which man and nature, spirit and matter are closely interwoven. AFT is not a natural science (like aromatherapy, for example), but a science of nature. The AFT can be understood as a metaphor for a 'holistic' method of nature and self-knowledge.

From the Ayurvedic theory of matter the idea of the structure of the USHMA (heat energy) in the human body was adopted. This mainly relates to emotions and the individual perception of the proportional existence of the elements in humans. (Earth, water, fire, air) The AFT method also takes into account the possibility of these elements being transformed into one another. Based on this understanding, I am then able to choose the fragrances which I use as basic notes in your bespoke/individual Compositions. Before you take your personal perfume home, you will be offered a round of basic notes. This allows me to create a perfume report for you, based on your spontaneous perceptions, your individual experience, the impact of the fragrances in your limbic, emotional and physical systems.
This allows you to go on a very unique scent journey which will awaken visual impressions such as colours, landscapes, feelings, memories, associations or scenes."

When we left Yogesh, I discussed my experience with Anita Ratschiner. We were both convinced that this was a rare ability of clear smelling. I had never come across anyone who didn't work in the spiritual area who had such a gift.

I loved the idea of a personal perfume that was actually based on my very own personal scent. Every perfume holds fragrances of the highest quality and comes in a beautiful bottle.
Yogesh is a true gem when it comes to the world of perfumes. His shop is located in Vienna and his individual perfumes start at 580, Euro.

Senses trigger strong emotional responses inside of us. It is even said that they create memories for a lifetime and we will never forget them. We can use this to our advantage and use this in the training of our personal psychic abilities.

### **Exercise:**

To train your clairscent ability, but also to help you to develop your sense of smell, I invite you to go out and get at least five different essential oil testers (Doterra or Young living are really good quality) Once you get them, sit down in your sacred space and smell one after the other.

Take notes with each smell of what comes to your mind – feelings, memories, colours, pictures etc.

One oil after another. This will really make your day!

*Yogesh and his
Perfumes
Photo credit:
www.diefotografin.at*

# Part III – Advancing in Your Journey

## 3.1 How to train your psychic abilities:

There are several ways and possibilities for training your psychic abilities. All of them will offer a stepping stone and different forms of experience on your way to the next level. During my personal path in discovering and developing my gifts, I tried many different routes and some of them served me more than others. It really depends on where you are heading and what your goal is. You might also find yourself moving back and forth between different pathways to get the best results. I came to the conclusion that if you ask yourself a few basic questions, it helps you to find your path.

<u>1. Do you think you have a solid foundation?</u>

If yes, look at more advanced courses. If you are not sure, focus on building the right foundation before moving forward.

<u>2. Do you like learning at your own pace or do you prefer set times and dates?</u>

If you enjoy learning at your own pace you want to consider a home study or online course. If you prefer set days, then workshops or set day courses may be for you.

<u>3. Do you like learning alone, with a partner, in small or large groups?</u>

If you like learning by yourself, a home study or online course can be useful. This way you have more freedom. There are often study groups connected to a home study course in which you can meet other students, exchange progress and ask questions. Local development classes or workshops might be for you if you like smaller groups. If you prefer larger groups, residential courses or workshops, as well as some online courses, may be for you.

<u>4. Do you have a specific subject in mind that you want to learn about?</u>

If so, look into intensive or in-depth courses, consider 1-2-1 Tuition with a Mentor or Teacher.

<u>5. Do you want to build a career or is it just a hobby (for now)?</u>

If you want to build a career, do more research to find the best courses available. If it's just a hobby then do what feels right for you at that time.

6. How much are you able/willing to pay?

A small or limited budget is great for some online or home study courses because there is no extra cost to get to the venue or stay overnight.
A bigger budget allows you to take residential courses with overnight stays, maybe something to consider if you're thinking about more intensive and in-depth courses.
A big budget can allow you to take up some residential courses overseas.
Just keep in mind that not everything that is expensive means quality, sometimes there are good courses for reasonable prices. There is often the opportunity to pay in instalments as well.

7. What is the most important about your training?

a) Good quality teaching
b) Well priced teaching within your budget
c) Famous, well-known teacher

See who and what resonates with you. Don't get blinded by the light just because someone is famous or people tend to follow a certain teacher. Additionally, I found that good knowledge doesn't always need to be expensive, you just need to know where to look. At the end of the day it's your energy, determination, willpower and effort that determines your personal success and growth.

**Open Circles (approx. 1.5 – 2 hours per meeting):**

These circles are very common within the UK and mostly held at Spiritualist Churches. Most open circles take place on a weekly basis and normally on an evening. Some open circles are held on weekends but that is individually decided by each church. Everyone is welcome to join for a small fee to be paid on the day. Check the internet for times and dates or contact the church directly. This can be a good chance to experience how other people work and to get the chance to get up and work yourself (if you wanted to). However, I found that a lot of open circles are not for development as such. If you ever want to work in a Spiritualist Church as a Spiritualist Medium then this is a good chance to meet new people or just to put yourself out there. Many circles are not run by teachers but by their members of the church. Some have good training and some don't. This will limit your progress at some point but you will gain courage and experience by getting up and working in front of others.

**Development Classes (approx. 2 hours per meeting):**

Similar to open circles these classes are held on a weekly or monthly basis in Spiritualist Churches. The focus in development classes is more on progressing with your psychic abilities. Development classes can offer a great opportunity for beginners to explore their potential. I also started in Development Classes when I visited England for my training. A friend took me to classes in York with Garry Brian Shirley and I benefited greatly from his insights and from meeting like-minded people. However, similar to open circles, the development classes are not always run by qualified teachers. It depends on the area you are in and what kind of teaching the church provides. Nevertheless, the classes are affordable and everyone is welcome. Some classes are closed groups over a certain period of time. The Spiritualist National Union (SNU) aims to provide structured and qualified training throughout. It is not an obligation to have a certificate to teach in churches which means the standard of teaching might vary. Of course, you can find development classes in any well-being centre or other spiritual centres and you will get good training dependent on the standard of the teacher.

**Workshops:**

Workshops can take place online, as residential, in a spiritualist centre, well-being hub or in Spiritualist Churches. Often, they are offered by more qualified teachers for a reasonable price. Most of the workshops are a one-off or a one-day event. Most workshops are focused on a specific subject and it can be a good opportunity to meet new people, make friends and learn something new. The quality of the teaching will depend on the teacher's knowledge, experience and ability to help other students develop. Prices vary with the area, the venue, teacher and subject.

**Online Courses:**

Online courses are popping up like mushrooms out of the ground. Especially in these rather challenging times of 2020, online courses have reached new levels of demand. Nearly everyone seems to offer something online and such courses are therefore covering all sorts of subjects. The great thing about online courses is that you can actually stay in the comfort of your own home, rather than needing to travel somewhere. Most online courses are held at a fixed date or time, some of them are even pre-recorded and if you can't attend at the fixed time then you get a link with the recording.

The pitfall with online courses can be that there could be technical issues with the internet connection. Additionally, many online courses don't give out any written content so it's all up to you to write notes while the course is running. Online courses offer great value and allow you to absorb teachings from all over the world. This is a great opportunity to listen to online talks and teachings and gain some inspiration or new ideas.

The teaching, lecture, is often free but at the end you are asked to sign up for a course that costs you a bit more. Of course, many offer community-based memberships and Q&A Sessions which maybe justifies the price at some point. Unless you are able to download the recording, then it's only available for that moment in time. Personally, I like things that I can refer back to rather than needing to turn on my computer to see them. I also sometimes feel that sitting too much in front of a computer screen emanates a lot of EMF which can lead to anxiety and nervous tension.

**Offline/Home Study Course/Self Study:**

Home Study Courses, I just love them! A great opportunity to learn something, but at your own pace and time. It's affordable and you receive written material which you can fall back on. I like the flexibility of Home Study Courses, which allows students to study anywhere and at any time. If you find the right teacher, you can really benefit from such an opportunity. Especially for psychic development, I think this option offers better opportunities than solely participating in online training. Many teachers offer home study courses for a reasonable price. Additionally, there are 1-2-1 Tuition Sessions available in which you can get individual and in-depth teaching. You can book them whenever you need them or have the spare money. Many home study courses are linked with a Facebook community/group or membership portals which you can join to meet other students, exchange progress, ask questions and share ideas.

There are different forms of Home Study Courses and some offer a certificate of completion at the end of the course, after you have gone through a final test in which you prove that you have understood the learning.

**Private 1-2-1 Tuition:**

Allows you to book a teacher or mentor on an hourly basis to help you with your personal development. A great opportunity for those who are serious about their progress and independent enough to put into place what they learnt. The great thing is that you can connect with any teacher, no matter where you are in the world.
Prices will vary depending on who you want to learn from. A 1-2-1 Tuition Session can be helpful to ask certain questions, raise specific issues or focus on the next individual step in your development. I love 1-2-1 Sessions because the teacher just focuses on me. For the last three years or so I have mostly only taken 1-2-1 Sessions with great teachers to make sure I progress in the right direction.
Most 1-2-1 Teaching Sessions are based around the student's personal stage of development at that time. Many teachers or coaches offer packages of three or six sessions which can save you some further money. This also makes sure that you progressed and benefited from the session.

**Life Itself:**

Well, life itself is probably still the greatest teacher. There are plenty of opportunities in everyday life which will challenge you to apply your new wisdom. You can also ask friends and family to support you. In the end, it's the energy and determination that you put in that really will make you move forward. Learning opportunities are plenty if we choose them when they present themselves.

**3.2 Forms of Expression:**

This book was created with the intent to support you in discovering your very own psychic potential. Like every teacher, the progress of my students is very close to my heart. I love seeing other people grow and unfold their authentic self when they are finally on their path of self-realisation. I also know that we can only find the truth ourselves and no one can do that for us. To have a guide, teacher or mentor along the path is valuable and sometimes even necessary. However, a mentor can only guide along the way – it's up to you what you actually take from this guidance.

I want to inspire you to grow out of old and limiting belief systems so that you can finally start unlocking your psychic potential. In this way, you will realize who you really are. How you express this potential is totally up to you and there are endless forms and no fixed path.

Please keep in mind that the forms of expression which are mentioned in this book are related to direct spiritual work. This doesn't mean that you can't choose any other field of work or expression that appeals to you. I encourage you to think outside of the box and follow your intuition. All I do is show you how to unfold and unlock this intuition so its messages are much clearer for you to understand. Developing your psychic potential is a path to finding a true and authentic expression of your innermost self. This doesn't necessarily mean that you need to become a Medium or a psychic artist. It means to become aware of a quality inside of you that you previously didn't know you had. The further you explore these qualities, the more you will find the right expression for you.

*Unlocking your Psychic Potential* is a tool, a method that will help you to go beyond what you thought you are and enter into a place of all that you could become. Enjoy the journey.

Try the exercise below to narrow down your own preferred form of expression!

# Forms of Expression Quiz:

### A. What do you get most excited about?

1. Giving other people advice
2. Helping others heal
3. Connecting with the spirit guide
4. Working on your own issues
5. Capturing real evidence for life after death.

### B. Which saying fits with you the most?

1. You like to dive deep
2. You are a critical thinker
3. You enjoy the company of others
4. You love healing energies
5. You like to assist others in their grieving process.

### C. Life after death

1. Is a possibility
2. You had a near death experience
3. You need more evidence for that
4. At the moment this is not important to you
5. You have received messages from a loved one.

### D. When you perceive information

1. You know the difference whether from spirit or from other people
2. You are confident about the meaning
3. You see similarities with your own experience
4. This occurs to you more in dreams
5. You have not really an idea what they mean.

### E. Do you…

1. Have a deep desire to help others?
2. Think you can distinguish between dead and living energy?
3. Enjoy visiting haunted sites and investigating?
4. Want to learn how to communicate with the spirit world?
5. Want to uncover shadow aspects that are hidden inside of you?

**F. Your main motivation for psychic development at the moment is:**

1. Personal healing
2. Finding out who you truly are
3. Convincing yourself about life after death
4. Wanting to find out if ghosts truly exist and to communicate with them
5. Discovering your own potential.

**G. If you had one super power it would be:**

1. Mind Reading
2. Communicating with the deceased
3. Knowing what the future holds
4. Helping lost souls to cross over
5. Being able to heal others.

**H. What do you like learn more about?**

1. Crystals
2. Automatic Writing
3. Technical Equipment
4. Tarot Cards
5. Drum and Rattle.

**I. Which places do you prefer?**

1. Wild places in nature
2. Churches
3. Castles and graveyards
4. Temples
5. Places with high energy.

**J. Which term describes you best at the moment?**

1. Curious
2. Relaxed
3. Nervous
4. Confused
5. Lost.

You can calculate your points at page 170 and find out what form of expression suits you at the moment.

# Forms of Expression – Test Results

## Paranormal Investigator (0 – 30 points):

A Paranormal Investigator is a person who visits different locations which are reported to be experiencing unexplained activity or phenomena. This can be castles, houses, properties, war memorials etc. However, a paranormal investigator can also investigate UFO Sightings, Demonological appearances and other unexplained happenings. Some paranormal investigators like to go deeper into the study of Parapsychology, others add Space Clearing and removal of negative energy to their work repertoire.

A Paranormal Investigator collects scientific data through several means, such as technical equipment which could confirm the existence of a spirit or life after death. In this way, he/she tries to find a rational explanation for what is happening at these locations. Some Paranormal Investigators are more trained than others and additionally possess knowledge of Parapsychology which gives them the advantage of being able to distinguish between certain paranormal phenomena. Those people are mostly aware of the difference between the residual and non-residual energy of places and can tell the difference. However, most of the Paranormal Investigators which are known to us via television series are more like Ghost Hunters. There is nothing wrong with this, as those people still use technical equipment to explain certain phenomena, but sadly they are often missing out on real evidence.

Paranormal Investigation is an important part of 'spiritual' work and it can be a very interesting hobby. It can also be a rather unusual job for people who are interested in the paranormal and the world beyond.

Some Paranormal Investigators also train in removing negative energy from places, as well as learning how to cross over lost souls if they feel that is part of their purpose. Good and solid training is important to protect oneself and others from the energies you might get in touch with.

A paranormal investigator needs to know about the regulations in place at each location before investigating. For this reason, it's important to check and read local laws on the property you want to investigate, no matter its land, country, state, county, city etc. and to stay up to date with any legal requirements regarding the pursuance of your hobby.

A very famous and extremely good Paranormal Investigator was Harry Price. He investigated hundreds upon hundreds of places as well as working with mediums such as Eileen Garrett. You can find out more about him and his life work at: **www.harrypricewebsite.co.uk**

*Harry Price and his most famous case, "Borley Rectory". He investigated this place over a period of ten years. Public domain 2020*

If you are in the USA and are looking for a more modern Paranormal Investigator you could check out John Zaffis.

**Ufology** is the investigation of UFOs, or Unidentified Flying Objects, by people known as Ufologists. This phenomenon of strange airships, defeating the laws of gravity with their speed and manoeuvrability, has been occurring across the world throughout history, and is depicted in art from ancient civilisations such as the Sumerians, Greeks, Romans and Egyptians, and also in 20th century incidents such as the case of the 'foo fighters', reported by allied air forces in WWII. There is also the Kenneth Arnold incident, where he saw nine blue, glowing objects travelling an estimated 1700 mph in a 'V' formation in June 1947. Ufologists tend to study phenomena with links to UFOs such as cattle mutilations, crop circles, alien abductions and implants, as well as looking into conspiracy theories such as the Roswell Incident and the Area 51 alien rumours.

**Parapsychology** is the study of psychic phenomena at a scientific level, looking at subjects such as E.S.P. (Extra Sensory Perception), reported cases of telepathy, reincarnation, precognition, clairvoyance, telekinesis and psychometry, as well as other paranormal claims such as NDEs, or Near Death Experiences, synchronicity and claims of apparitions and hauntings. It became popular in the 1850s when several well-respected scientists, Robert Hare, Alfred Russel Wallace, and Sir William Crookes, came together to investigate the claims of Spiritualist Mediums. This in turn caught the interest of others, some being a group of scholars, Henry Sedgwick, Frederic William Henry Myers, and Edmund Gurney, who later founded the Society for Physical Research in 1882, which still continues to this day.


**Demonology** is quite simply the study of demons and demonic activity, the Devil, Satan, as well as possessions and exorcisms. There are thought by some to be many kinds of demons, including human and non-human souls, or discarnate spirits which have never been in a human body. Humans have believed in evil since the early beginning of human civilization, and we haven't lost our interest. Since modern horror movies and TV shows have depicted demons taking over humans and wreaking havoc among us, or bringing Hell on earth wherever they roam, more and more people have become interested in the subject. Though saying this, not every culture believes that all demons are evil. Some pre-Christian and non-Christian cultures believed, and still do believe, that demons are not necessarily good or evil.

**Space Clearing**
For centuries, the ancient art of Space Clearing has been used in many cultures such as those in Bali, Morocco, Peru, and India, and is still utilized across the globe. As it says in the title, this is the clearing of a space, but on an energetic level. Like dust accumulates due to everyday activities, it's the same with energy and this needs to be cleansed regularly as it becomes stagnant or negative over time. This could be due to several reasons, such as poor energetic circulation, divorce, negative people, death, illness – both physical and mental – addictions or spirit entities. There is also precautional Space Clearing, which you would

perform at a new home or property, work office, or when buying a second-hand vehicle, to clear away the historical imprints of others. There are several differing methods of Space Clearing, such as smudging, using sound and music, resins with charcoal, and crystals, to name but a few.

*1l) smudging tools (Palo Santo & Sage)*

**Cryptozoology**

Cryptozoology is the search for and study of animals, known as Cryptids, whose existence or survival is disputed or unsubstantiated. Examples of such Cryptids are: the Jersey Devil, Bigfoot, Yeti, Mothman, Skunk Ape and Yeren. There have been some creatures who were on the Cryptids list which were proven real, such as the Okapi of the Congo (which looks like a cross between a Zebra and a Giraffe), the Western lowland Gorilla of Africa (which before being known to the western world, was just a tale told for centuries of giant apes living in the jungles), and the giant squid (which was only seen live for the first time in 2005). This creature can grow to forty plus feet in length and is possibly the inspiration for the Norwegian myth of the Kraken. One of the most well-known Cryptids is the Loch Ness Monster. Whether it exists is subject to discussion, but the fascination is still there and some of you might enjoy the hunt for this rather unusual figure!

*1m) The Loch Ness Monster*

**Your next steps could be:**

- Take part in a group paranormal investigation
- Read a book about hauntings
- Read a book about Harry Price (one of the best investigators who ever existed)
- Contact a Paranormal Investigator to cleanse your house
- Book a private Paranormal Investigation for your property
- Join or research the Society for Psychical Research
- Listen to lectures on the paranormal
- Research the job description of a Paranormal Investigator / Parapsychologist
- Check out RBR Paranormal Investigations on Facebook – they have great articles about the paranormal
- Join the Ghost Club in London
- Read up on the Parapsychology Foundation or Institute for Noetic Science
- Book a trip to Scotland and look for the Loch Ness Monster
- Ask your local priest uncomfortable questions about demons and exorcism! :-)

## Psychic (31 – 45 points):

The psychic expression is something that resonates with you the most at the moment.
Psychic work is a very interesting form of spiritual work which offers a variety of different expressions.
The best starting point is to follow your passion and you will easily find an expression. Ask yourself:

- Do I like Tarot Cards?
- Am I creative?
- Could I imagine giving Readings to others?
- Would I be interested in investigating haunted places?
- Do I want to use my psychic abilities in the field of healing?

Whatever you choose, your psychic development will teach you how to use your inborn abilities – to learn to absorb and interpret what lies beyond the normal senses.
The most known form of psychic expression is a Psychic Medium or a Tarot Card Reader. This is a very active state of spiritual work and includes working with other people.
Working as a Psychic Medium or Tarot Card Reader enables you to sense, see, hear and feel the past, present and future potential of people or situations, and allows you to blend with their soul.
This can be of great help for those in need of clarity and focus. However, it is important to understand that we need to go through stages of personal development to be of good value in giving insights to others.

## Tarot Card Reader (Psychic)

A very old form of divination which has been around for hundreds of years. Similar to a Psychic Medium, a Tarot Card Reader works with the living energy of the sitter. In this form of psychic expression, the energy of the sitter is made visible through the laying out of the Tarot Cards or Oracle Cards.
This field of work doesn't only allow you to make the sitter's energy more visible, additionally the Tarot Card Reader uses less of their own energy to gain insights. Furthermore, the Tarot Card Reader gets inspired (triggered) by the cards to give intuitive guidance on a situation.
There are different forms of reading the cards and making an interpretation and it requires some skills and training to do so. A Tarot Card Reader should always work with a deck of cards that resonates with

them and there are so many wonderful decks now available. The quality of the reading will be determined by the overall knowledge of the Tarot Card Reader and his/her intuitive skill to relate the cards to the current situation of a person.

A psychic reading with or without cards always presents the current energetic circumstances of a person and often mirrors what people think or feel. A Psychic or Tarot Card Reader is not a fortune teller. He/she can't make predictions, but they can show future potential. Ultimately, destiny lies in everyone's own hands and in the choices they make. A good Psychic or Tarot Card Reader reminds the client of their self-responsibility and follows ethical and moral standards in their practice.

*1n)*

## Psychic Artist

A Psychic Artist tunes into the energy field of his/her sitter, or blends with the soul of the sitter, and will create a painting by doing so. The colours which are used in the picture express the sitter's life and circumstances. Normally, the Psychic Artist creates a painting while the sitter is present and at the same time gives interpretations about the sitter's life. However, in many cases it is also possible that the picture is created from a distance, and the recording of the reading as well as the picture will be sent to the client. This can be a nice way to receive something very unique to hold on to after you have had a psychic reading. There are different names for these pictures, such as Aura-graph, Soul-pictures or Spirit Guide Painting.

1o)  Pictures by Swiss Psychic Artist – Claudia Hollenweger

## **Spirit Guide Painting**

Some Psychic Artists are specialized in painting people's spirit guides. In such cases, Psychic Artists will tune into the sitter's energy and receive information about the spirit guide who is working with them. Keeping in mind that we can have more than just one spirit guide, some people have teams of guides. Additionally, as much as I like the idea, we also need to be mindful that the painting might not reflect our personal idea of the spirit guide. At the end of the day, we know that spirit guides have no forms as such and can also shape shift between forms. They might present themselves in a certain way so it's more recognisable for yourself.

*1p) Pictures by UK based Psychic Artist – Julie Eventsartist*

Getting your Spirit Guide painted can be an interesting session. However, keep in mind that you can have many spirit guides and what you see might not look like the one you imagined. This does not mean that it's not your spirit guide, but rather is one of many guiding you.

**Aura Photography**

Aura Photography Sessions takes place in person to capture your Aura on camera and offer you insight and guidance into your well-being and energy. The Aura is our spiritual body that surrounds our physical body. It is like a bubble of protective energy that most of us can't see, but which many of us can feel.

Can you recall a moment when you have had someone stood behind you? Perhaps you couldn't see them, but you intuitively knew they were there. That's your Aura, letting you know that someone is stood in your energy field.

Aura photography offers you the unique opportunity to see your spiritual energy and discover who you are on the inside. Your Aura colours also reflect where you are in your consciousness and your spiritual, physical, and emotional awareness. Aura Photography works through using the science of biofeedback, colour therapy, and energy medicine – it's fascinating.

*1q) Photos taken by Holistic Therapist and Aura photographer, Deanna Thomas*

## Psychic Medium in Paranormal Investigations

A Psychic Medium can be very helpful or useful during paranormal investigations because they can pick up atmospheric impressions. Such intuitive information can express itself in the form of scenes, feelings, noises etc. If a tragic event such as a murder, unexpected death, torture or abuse has happened, it will leave a strong imprint in the 'aura' of the place. This is called residual energy (or atmospheric impression). A Psychic Medium can tap into this energy and re-live the event energetically. A recalling of energetic memory or any leftover energy is not 'SPIRIT COMMUNICATION'. Real spirit communication is more than a psychic impression. The spirit in that case will respond intelligently to questions that have been asked, while residual energy does not. The lack of training and understanding in this field often leads to false impressions and builds up an idea of spirit commutation that is not real.
This type of work is not for everybody and a procedure of cleansing, protection and grounding should be done before and after visiting any haunted places. Otherwise, you might end up with an energetic attachment which can have an impact on your personal life.

## My Real Life Story:

The strongest psychic impression I ever received was during my visit to Culloden Battlefield in Scotland. While we were walking around the field, I suddenly became aware via my clairaudient ability people screaming, before my inner eye scenes of battle arose and I quickly found myself quite overwhelmed by so many happenings at the same time. Not to mention the pain, the rage and the overall fight these men went through.
I also perceived many psychic impressions on other paranormal investigations which I did together with RBR Paranormal, but none of them were as vivid as the battlefield in Scotland.

## Psychic Detective

Psychic detectives use their abilities to find missing people. Most psychic detectives work together with the police, though some of them might be hired by private people too.

Dependent on their psychic ability and training, the psychic detective is either able to trace the last steps of the missing person, give clues about their current location and/or speak about the details of what happened. Other psychic detectives might be able to take on the view of the murderer, abuser etc. and through this they can give clues as to what happened.

This work holds some real challenges and it is emotionally very demanding. You will be dealing with a lot of trauma, loss and pain. In the long term, this can lead to personal problems in your own life if you don't find ways to deal with it.
Putting your own life on hold while working on a case is only one factor to consider.
If anyone wants to do this, they need to be properly trained in how to perform remote viewing, connect with the missing person or the victim, take on the perspective of the abuser, abductor or murderer and know how to use psychometry, photos, automatic writing and so on to help the case. I have worked on a few cases and found the work incredibly demanding and traumatising. People underestimate the work of a psychic detective and the consequences which come with it. However, if someone feels called to do such work and learn how to do it, then they 'need' to find a good teacher who knows what they are talking about. Not only do you need to learn how to solve such cases, but also how to look after yourself before, after and during the case.
The British medium Tony Stockwell worked as a psychic detective and had his own academy.

### **Your next steps could be:**

- Train your abilities, with the right teacher, to the next level
- Use Tarot cards on a daily basis for personal guidance
- Read books on psychic development
- Start some therapy with a good therapist
- Look into chakra work and development
- Look into deeper forms of healing or other forms of psychic expression (Art, writing, speaking, psychometry, aura reading, paranormal investigation, channelling, spiritualist mediumship, trance work)
- Book yourself a Psychic Reading or Tarot Card Reading
- Get your Aura photographed
- Get yourself an Aura Graph Reading and picture.

*1r) Cemetery Picture*

## Spiritualist Medium (46 – 60 points):

You are more drawn to the work of a Spiritualist Medium. You are seeking evidence for life after death and want to help other people in their grieving process.

A Spiritualist Medium connects with the spirit world. Therefore, they do not read the auric field from another person but rather receive information from another plane. Thus a Spiritualist Medium's main goal is to give evidence for life after death and bring messages from deceased loved ones.

This job is not for everybody because you are working with 'dead' energy rather than with 'living' energy. A good Spiritualist Medium should provide information about gender, relationship to the sitter, some shared memories, a name, or another piece of information which clearly identifies the other person in the spirit world to the sitter. It takes years of good training to achieve a recognisable level of good Spiritualist Medium expression. In the UK, the SNU provides the highest standard of education in this field.

Spiritualist Mediums can work in public, mostly on stage or in Spiritualist Churches, in which they demonstrate their mediumship. Others might prefer to work more privately – in such cases the Spiritualist Mediums would offer 1-2-1 Sittings/Readings (Evidential

Sitting) to their clients. Some Spiritualist Mediums also offer Reading Parties in which they would go to the client's house and give readings to them and some of their friends. You will need to find out what works for you and in which way you would like to progress.

On the path to becoming a Spiritualist Medium, you might also discover a new expression of Mediumship that you didn't know existed (such as different forms of Trance or Physical Mediumship).

*Scottish Spiritualist Medium and Tutor at the Arthur Findlay College, Bill Thompson, at a public Demonstration of Mediumship in Switzerland.*

### **Automatic Writer Medium (Spiritualist Medium)**

Automatic Writing (Trance State) is a great expression for all those who like to write. It's different than normal writing because it requires some openness and training. There have been amazing automatic writing mediums who brought messages from beyond and evidence for life after death. Inspirational writing, in which we allow a higher power to work through us to pass on words of wisdom, philosophy or healing, is also possible. It can be a fascinating experience if we know how to do it.

In the movie *Kardec*, the two little daughters of his friend show incredible talent in automatic writing while a spirit works through them. You can also look into Leonora Piper who was an American Trance Medium who offered readings in writing.

*1s) Leonora Piper, 1922*

## **Art and Spiritualist Mediumship**

There are Spiritualist Mediums who are artists as well and use these abilities in their private readings or public demonstrations. Other than the Psychic Artist, who connects with the soul energy of the sitter, a Spiritualist Artist will connect with a deceased soul from the beyond and draw him/her during the reading or demonstration. In this way it can be used as evidence for survival after death, as well as the sitter being able recognise his/her loved one. If you have ever attended a public demonstration with someone drawing a loved one from the spirit world you know it's an amazing experience.

This picture was drawn by Elke Schneider, who is a Spiritualist Medium, Psychic Artist and Tarot Card Reader, during a private sitting. After the private sitting the client showed her a photograph of the person who just came through to communicate. The resemblance is fascinating.

*1t) Painting by Elke Schneider*

## Trance Medium (Spiritualist Medium)

A Trance Medium is a form of mental mediumship in which the spirit will take over the Medium's body and work through it. This takes years of training and of building a connection and rapport with the spirit world to allow full expression. There are different trance states that need to be mastered, and a Medium needs to sit for Trance regularly. Over time, the spirit world will try to use and manipulate the voice box for Trance speaking, the body and hands for healing or psychic surgery, and the mind for Trance healing.

There have been some incredible cases documented for Trance Mediumship, in which the Medium even spoke other languages or the voice of a loved one who had already passed away clearly came through. Someone interested in such phenomena should start learning and experimenting with different Trance States. Exploring Trance States will go hand in hand with exploring oneself. A good mentor/teacher can help with this.

Normally, if having been in real Trance State, the Medium has no recall afterwards of what happened during the Trance State. If working with others or in public, the Trance Medium will always need another helper to make sure everything is okay. The Trance Medium puts themselves into a vulnerable space and therefore needs to make sure they have other people around who are looking after them during that time.

## Further research

You could look into:
Andrew Jackson Davis – *The Magic Staff*
Eileen Garrett – Any of her books (Trance Mediumship)
Isa Northgate

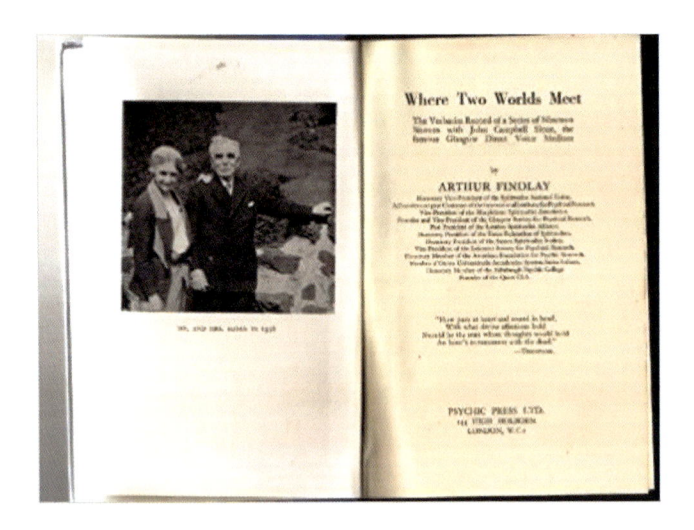

*1u) John Campbell Sloan with his wife in 1946 – Investigated by Arthur Findlay – Where Two Worlds Meet (Spirit Voice Phenomenon)*

**Next steps could be:**

- Look for Spiritualist Medium courses
- Take part in an open circle
- Start exploring working with psychometry to trigger connection with the spirit world
- Practice Sitting in the Power to build up energetic stamina
- Intensify your clair sense ability
- Learn better forms of Spiritualist Medium expression and learn how to give better evidence
- Practice giving better messages to people
- Read a book about grief, life after death
- Study books from other Spiritualist Mediums (the SNU Website offers a good variety)
- Check out our Self-Study course to unlock your psychic potential.

# Learn more about
# "UNLOCKING YOUR PSYCHIC POTENTIAL"

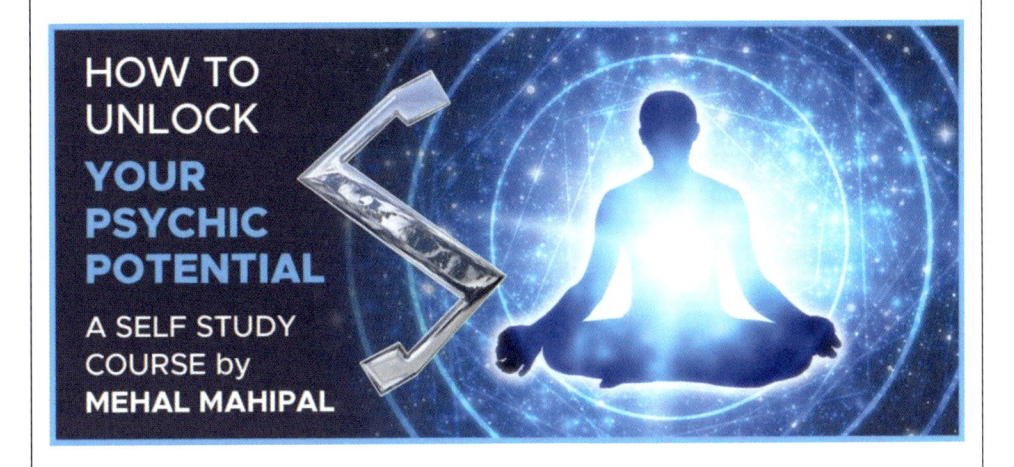

12 Video/Audio Lectures & Printable Transcripts
Proven methods & interactive assessments

**Bonus:** over **180 minutes** of Audio Meditations

**Learn at your own pace
with**

www.unlockingpsychicpotential.com

## Healing Expression (61 – 75 points):

You should explore healing as your current state of expression. This more passive state of working allows healing energies from the universe, spirit, and other dimensions to flow into the other person's body, mind and spirit. The ability to heal is inborn in all of us, however it still takes training to be able to heal others and oneself.

There are guidelines and procedures that the healer should learn about to qualify themselves to practice any healing arts. Learning healing can also be a great beginning for many different forms of self-development and further spiritual growth.

To know how to heal is a great power which we should all learn and possess, so that we know how to help ourselves and others.

## Reiki Healer

The most common form of energy healing which is taught all over the world is Reiki. Originally developed by Dr. Usui, learning Reiki will help you to step into the realms of energy healing and can also open other doors for you.

There are now different forms of Reiki available, but originally it was brought into this world by Dr. Usui and his line of Usui Shiki Ryoho Reiki. There are Levels 1 and 2 and a Master Degree.

Level 1 forms the basics and will also teach you how to heal yourself first. Level 2 allows you to heal others and the Master Degree forms the foundation of passing Usui Reiki knowledge on to other people.

*1v) Self-healing, an important Reiki practice*

## Spiritual Healer

A form of healing that is mostly taught in Spiritualist Churches but also in other spiritual movements. Any form of healing that is based on faith in a higher power or source can be put into this category. Prayer healing, faith healing or healing with spirits from another dimension could fit into this category.

## Trance Healer

In this case of healing, the healer enters another state of consciousness. Normally, if trained well, he/she will be able to enter different forms of Trance State. This form of healing is very well known in the Spiritualist Movement. The Medium allows the spirit to possess them and give healing or even conduct psychic surgery. Originally this is the oldest form of healing and has been practised by shamans, medicine men and women throughout the centuries.

## Further Research:

Stephen Turoff – Psychic Surgeon

## Healing with Creative Art

There are very gifted Healers and Artists out there who combine these two elements and create something truly powerful and unique. Healing Art is a form of healing in which the healing energies are directly channelled into a painting which can then be passed on to the person in need. In this way, the healing energy keeps radiating from the painting and this makes it a great gift for people. You can place powerful healing art into your home or workplace and absorb the healing energy every time you are in that space. Some artists use certain materials or colours, symbols and other markings to enhance healing qualities.

As an artist you can also create healing sculptures, poems, stories and any other crafty things.

*Spirit Art by Elke Schneider*

**Your next steps could be:**

- Book yourself a healing session (in person or via a distance)
- Look for a healing course near you
- Train your psychic abilities to enhance healing potential and gain more clarity on ailments
- Use Tarot cards for healing
- Practice (learn) distant healing
- Learn a new form of healing that allows healing on a deeper level
- Specialize in certain areas for healing (pain relief, mental health, certain areas of the body etc.)
- Look into different tools you could use for your healing practice such as nutrition, essential oils, massage, prayer, blessings, astrology etc.

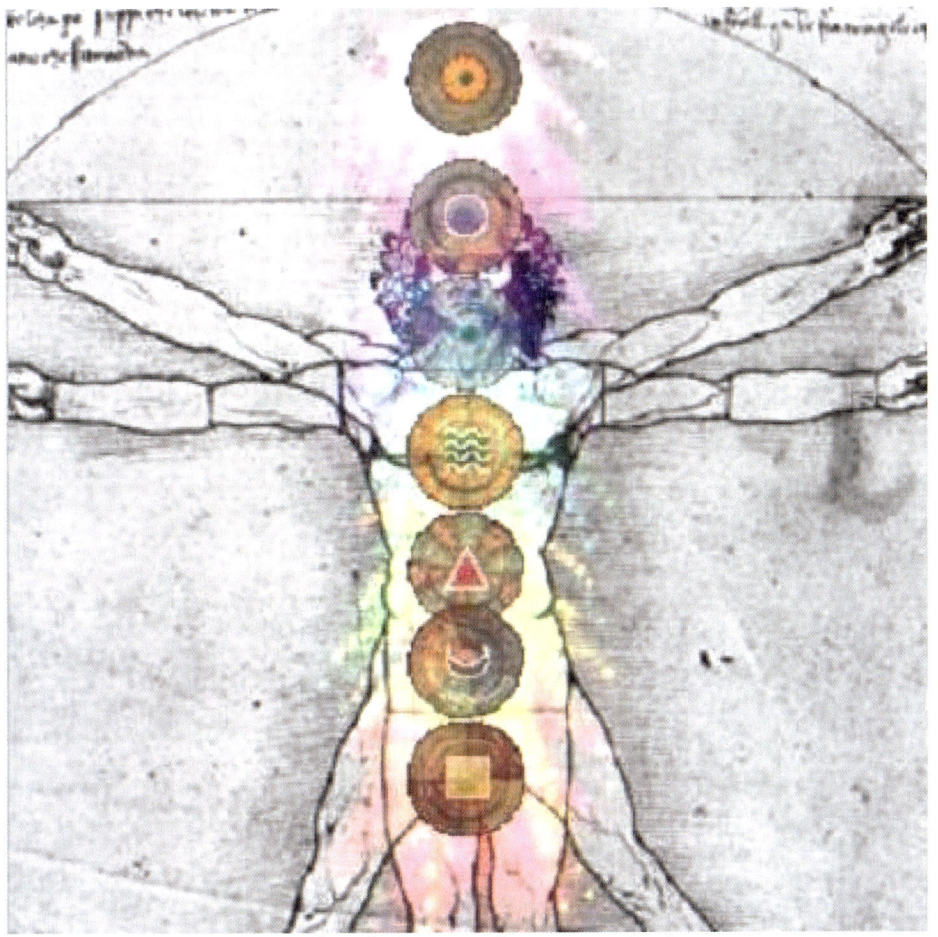

1w) The chakras in the energy body

## Shamanic Practitioner (76 – 100 points):

You are in a state in which you want to do some deep inner work that helps you to discover hidden aspects of yourself. To become a Shamanic Practitioner it takes time, resilience, patience and the willingness to embrace one's own shadow.

Shamanic Practitioners have been around for thousands of years. Nearly every culture had their own medicine men and women who played an important part in bringing healing to the community. Shamans work with guides and spirits from other planes, but also receive power from animals and plants. Their wisdom is often passed down from one generation to the next within their lineage. Sacred rituals and plant medicine form an important part of their healing practice.

Shamanic healers have gone through years of initiation and training, working themselves through the wounded healer journey, confronting and releasing shadow aspects of themselves. They are close to nature, the embodiment of their work, and explore different Trance States through dance, music, movement or substances.

There are different lineages of shamanism and it is important if you want to set out on this journey to find one that works for you. Please don't experiment in inducing the Trance State with substances if you don't know what you are doing. Always consult a teacher before experimenting with things that you are not sure of. Shamanic work is deep shifting work and can lead to emotional and mental crisis if you don't have a mentor who can guide you through the difficult parts.

The shamanic path is different for everyone and has many different expressions. However a good shamanic practitioner training lasts between three and five years.

A safe way would perhaps be to experiment with ceremonial cacao – you can find a recipe and a whole article on how to do that on my website.

## To find out more about different types of Shamanism:

**Peruvian Shamanism:** Research Inca Shamanism or Qero Shamanism

**Chinese Shamanism:** Research Wu, Wuism or Hongshan culture

**Siberian Shamanism:** Research Buryats, Lake Baikal, Trans-Baikal, Tuva and Altai

**Native Americans:** Don't have shamanic views but have medicine men etc.

**African Shamanism:** Research traditional African healing

**Japanese Shamanism:** Research Shinto, blind fusha or yogensha.

**Herbalism:** This is the tradition of studying and using herbs for their healing properties. It is often found in traditional Shamanic healing and can be added to your list of training or interests if you walk this path.

**Healing the Earth:** The Shaman does not only communicate with spirits from the heavens but also with the spirits of the earth. He/She understands that every little thing on this earth has a soul. A part of Shamanic practice can be to heal the earth and restore wholeness. This depends on the lineage you choose and in which environment you are going to practice this art.

**Urban Shamanism:** There are Shamanic Practitioners who live in cities and practice their craft in urban areas. Gabriel Roth, the founder of the 5Rhythms Dance, always called herself an Urban Shaman and practised her art in many different locations and events.

**Other forms of Energy/Body Medicine:** There are many other forms of energy medicine which I have not included in this book and you can research these on the internet. There are plenty of resources and possibilities to find something that sparks your interest and ignites the fire in your soul.
Some of them are: Homeopath, Chiropractor, Osteopath, Aromatherapist, Massage therapist, Acupuncturist, Bach flower Remedy Therapist, Theta Healing, Quantum Healing, Astrologer with focus on Health and Medicine, Feng Shui Consultant, Reflexologist, Chinese Medicine Practitioner, Ayurveda Practitioner, Nutritional Therapist, Herbalist, Yoga Teacher, Qi Gong Teacher, Tai Chi Teacher, Crystal Healer, and so on….

*1x) Shamanic Drumming*

**Your next steps could be:**

- Read a book on Shamanic Healing and see which lineage you are drawn to
- Go out and connect with the elements
- Read a book on how to work with the Shadow
- Start exploring past lives
- Start tracing your lineage
- Look for a shamanic teacher
- Start looking into healing animals and the earth
- Do a cacao ceremony
- Look into Ceremonial Rituals such as for Blessings, Weddings and Funerals
- Start dancing and singing
- Look into Astrology (healing at the right time)
- Book yourself a Shamanic Healing session and experience its power.

# 3.3 15 Tools to start unlocking your Psychic Potential

Over all the years of my personal psychic development and research into psychic phenomena, I came across some very good and useful methods.
All of these techniques will assist you in developing your own potential. I have gathered some of my known techniques here to allow you to explore them at your own pace. Keeping in mind that there will be days when you will achieve great results and other days when you will struggle a little bit more. However, please remind yourself that on all of those days you are actually making progress.

## 1. Crystals:

Crystals can be a good tool to use in two different ways to enhance your psychic abilities.
You can either choose a specific crystal, which is said to have properties to help develop psychic potential, grounding, enhanced vision or healing. In this case you would make use of its properties to charge your psychic force or life force.
Another way would be that you use any crystals, hold them in your hand with your eyes closed and guess their specific properties. Be open to whatever comes into your mind, what you see, feel or hear and write it on a piece of paper. You can then check on the internet, in a book or your personal notes, if you were right about what you picked up.

*1y) Crystals*

## 2. Tarot and Oracle Cards:

I really love working with these. It's very important that you choose a deck that resonates with you. Connect with a daily card and listen to its intuitive guidance (this means not looking into a book for meaning). Write down your personal insights and meaning. This way you allow yourself to access more inspirational parts of yourself. You start building confidence in your intuition and personal wisdom. At the same time, you start building a relationship with your higher self.

Example of Astrology Tarot Cards I use in my 1-2-1 Readings:

### 3. Psychometry:

A powerful way to learn to read energy from an object. Ask a friend to assist you by giving you an object of someone who they know, but who is unknown to you. Hold the object in your hand, say what you feel or see and hear and check with your friend if that is correct. You can also write your insights down and check in with your friend afterwards.

### 4. Photo:

Ask someone to give you a picture of someone they know and then allow any impressions (clairvoyantly, clairaudiently, clairsentiently etc.) to come to you. Take the picture in both hands, speak about your insights or write them down to check afterwards with the person who handed you the picture.

### 5. Automatic Writing:

Take a pen and paper and just write down anything that comes to your mind. No matter if it makes sense or not. Just let the inspiration flow. Automatic writing is often done in a different state of consciousness such as the Trance State. By starting to just write what comes to mind you start preparing for future Trance Writing – in which you can either channel messages from your higher self, the universe, guides, spiritual beings or deceased loved ones.

### 6. Art:

Are you creative? Why not start expressing your abilities in a different way!
Choose any colours you feel drawn to and just paint, whatever comes to your mind. Stay open – let it flow. This is a very intuitive way to paint and doesn't require much skill. It's about learning to open up and allowing the colours to move you. Allow yourself to draw any shapes, forms, patterns, colours etc.

### 7. Colours:

Each colour carries a unique energy and meaning. Pick one colour at a time, hold it in your hand and write down anything that comes to your mind. What you see, feel or hear etc. A great way to learn to interpret colours in an intuitive way.

*1z) Colour Spiral*

## 8. Dreams:

Start a dream journal. Record what you dreamt in the morning right away after you have woken up. You'll be surprised what messages come through or possible precognitions, visions and insights you will receive. A very powerful and interesting way to explore the wisdom of altered states of consciousness.

## 9. Spirit Cabinet:

You can build a Spirit Cabinet and sit in it to feel the different energies. This can add something useful to your meditation practice, especially when you practice Sitting in the Power. However, the Spirit Cabinet can be used for healing, Trance Speaking as well as physical phenomena. Over time I have used it for different reasons in my workshops in Trance, Healing and also Overshadowing. Additionally, I have used it and still use it for certain paranormal experiments together with RBR Paranormal Investigations.

## 10. People:

Ask other people to allow you to read their energy. Just sit opposite the person, or do it via Skype or even without seeing each other (just allocate a time you both agree to). Write down all the things that come to your mind. Ask the person for feedback and if they understand anything that you have seen, felt or heard etc.

## 11. TV:

Believe it or not, but you can actually train your psychic abilities by watching TV. Choose a movie or series that you don't know but that speaks to you. Allow yourself to connect emotionally with the actors in the movie or series. Try now and again to guess what they will say next or what is going to happen. You will be surprised how this can actually enhance your abilities and you'll learn how to read energy. Once you are surprisingly right about stuff, your confidence will grow automatically.

## 12. Trance State:

Start experimenting with other states of consciousness through dance, movement, music and also meditation. Seek a teacher if you unsure on how to do that.

## 13. Reading and Inspiration:

Read inspiring books and stories. Allow poetry, philosophy, literature to resonate with your soul and inspire you in everyday life. Write down what this does to you, how you felt about it and which part of you was deeply moved, or didn't like it at all etc. It helps to connect with the soul energy and creates more resonance vibrations.

## 14. Meditation:

One of the most important ingredients for any psychic ability work. There are different forms of meditation that can help with your development. Most important are those which help you to become still and relaxed.

## 15. Flower Remedies (Bach) or Essential Oils

Choose a Flower Remedy whilst blindfolded. Hold it in your hand and absorb its energy. Become aware of what you see, hear or feel. What is the use of the remedy? Which ailments can be cured or helped by it? Do you get any pains in your body? Who should use the remedy? Record yourself speaking or write down your insights. Later on, compare your findings with the actual description of the remedy. You can do the same with essential oils.
This exercise will help you to gain inner knowing and enhances your psychic abilities. Additionally it also to create more rapport with certain

physical, mental or emotional problems which can help you if you want to become a healer and include this into your repertoire.

*Bach Flower Remedy by Pics by Fran, Pixabay, Feb 2021*

## Stages of Development Quiz Calculation and Answers:

### Calculating your points -

**A.**
1. Answer → 2
2. Answer → 5
3. Answer → 7
4. Answer → 5
5. Answer → 2

**B.**
1. Answer → 5
2. Answer → 2
3. Answer → 7
4. Answer → 5
5. Answer → 7

**C.**
1. Answer → 7
2. Answer → 5
3. Answer → 2
4. Answer → 2
5. Answer → 7

**D.**
1. Answer → 2
2. Answer → 5
3. Answer → 7
4. Answer → 2
5. Answer → 7

**E.**
1. Answer → 5
2. Answer → 2
3. Answer → 7
4. Answer → 2
5. Answer → 5

**F.**
1. Answer → 5
2. Answer → 7
3. Answer → 2
4. Answer → 7
5. Answer → 2

**G.**
1. Answer → 2
2. Answer → 5
3. Answer → 7
4. Answer → 5
5. Answer → 2

**H.**
1. Answer → 7
2. Answer → 5
3. Answer → 2
4. Answer → 5
5. Answer → 7

**I.**
1. Answer → 7
2. Answer → 2
3. Answer → 5
4. Answer → 7
5. Answer → 5

**J.**
1. Answer → 5
2. Answer → 2
3. Answer → 7
4. Answer → 5
5. Answer → 2

### Add all the points for the answers you have given together and find out your total:

### Points:

| | |
|---|---|
| 0 – 25 | Empath |
| 25 – 45 | Intuitive |
| 45 – 65 | Awakened Intuitive |

## Forms of Expression quiz calculation and answers:

### Calculating your points:

**A.**
1. Answer → 4
2. Answer → 8
3. Answer → 6
4. Answer → 10
5. Answer → 3

**B.**
1. Answer → 10
2. Answer → 3
3. Answer → 4
4. Answer → 8
5. Answer → 6

**C.**
1. Answer → 4
2. Answer → 10
3. Answer → 3
4. Answer → 8
5. Answer → 6

**D.**
1. Answer → 6
2. Answer → 10
3. Answer → 4
4. Answer → 8
5. Answer → 3

**E.**
1. Answer → 8
2. Answer → 4
3. Answer → 3
4. Answer → 6
5. Answer → 10

**F.**
1. Answer → 8
2. Answer → 10
3. Answer → 6
4. Answer → 3
5. Answer → 4

**G.**
1. Answer → 4
2. Answer → 6
3. Answer → 10
4. Answer → 3
5. Answer → 8

**H.**
1. Answer → 8
2. Answer → 6
3. Answer → 3
4. Answer → 4
5. Answer → 10

**I.**
1. Answer → 10
2. Answer → 6
3. Answer → 3
4. Answer → 8
5. Answer → 4

**J.**
1. Answer → 3
2. Answer → 8
3. Answer → 4
4. Answer → 6
5. Answer → 10

### Add all the points for the answers together and calculate your total:

### Points:

| | |
|---|---|
| 0 – 35 | Paranormal |
| 36 – 50 | Psychic |
| 51 – 65 | Spiritualist Medium |
| 66 – 80 | Healing Expression |
| 81 – 100 | Shamanic Practitioner |

# Book List for further Reading and Studies

## Mediumship & Spiritualism

*Adventures in the Supernormal,* Eileen J. Garrett, 1949
*A History of Mankind Volumes I and II,* Arthur Findlay, 1947
*Awareness,* Eileen J. Garrett, 1943
*D. D. Home – His life and Mission,* Sir Arthur Conan Doyle, 1921
*Eileen Garrett and the World Beyond the Senses*, Allan Angoff, William Morrow, 1974.
*Human Personality and its Survival after Physical Death,* Frederic W.H. Myers, 1903
*In the presence of White Feather,* Robert and Amanda Goodwin, 2004
*Memories and Adventures,* Arthur Conan Doyle, 1924
*Mountain Paths,* Maurice Maeterlinck, 1911
*My Life As a Search for the Meaning of Mediumship,* Eileen J. Garrett, 1939
*My Search for truth*, Horton, 1902
*On The Edge Of The Etheric: Being An Investigation Of Psychic Phenomena, in which Findlay examines the theory that spirits are linked to subatomic physics*, Arthur Findlay, 2010 (new edition)
*Our African Winter,* Arthur Conan Doyle, 1929
*Our American Adventure,* Arthur Conan Doyle, 1923
*Our Second American Adventure,* Arthur Conan Doyle, 1923
*Spiritualist Readers,* Arthur Conan Doyle, 1924
*Spiritual Steps on the spiritual level*, White Eagle, 2005
*Telepathy: In Search of a Lost Faculty*, Eileen J. Garrett, 1941

*The Case of Spiritualist Photography,* Arthur Conan Doyle, 1924
*The Coming of Fairies,* Arthur Conan Doyle, 1922
*The Edge of the Unknown,* Arthur Conan Doyle, 1930
*The Effect Of Religion On History* **(Booklet),** Arthur Findlay, 1953
*The History of Spiritualism,* Arthur Conan Doyle, 1926
*The Land of Mist,* Arthur Conan Doyle, 1926
*The New Revelation,* Arthur Conan Doyle, 1918
*The Torch Of Knowledge*, Arthur Findlay, 1996 (new edition)
*The Psychic Stream*, Arthur Findlay, 1939
*The Rock Of Truth, a history of the persecution of mediums by Christianity,* Arthur Findlay, 1933
*The Sense and Nonsense of Prophecy*, Eileen J. Garrett, 1960
*The Spirit's Book: The Classic Guide to Spiritism and the Spirit World*, Allan Kardec, 1857
*The Unfolding Universe or The Evolution of Man's Conception of His Place in Nature*, Arthur Findlay, 1935
*The Vital Message,* Arthur Conan Doyle, 1919
*The Way Of Life*, Arthur Findlay, 1996 (New edition)
*Wanderings of a Spiritualist,* Arthur Conan Doyle, 1921
*Where Two Worlds Meet,* about Findlay's encounters with the medium John Sloan, Arthur Findlay, 1951

## **Theosophy**

*Ancient Wisdom*, Annie Beasant, 1897
*Karma*, Annie Beasant, 1895
*Man and his bodies,* Annie Beasant, 1917
*Man visible and invisible*, Charles Leadbeater, 2006 (New edition)
*Telepathy,* Alice Bailey, 1950
*The inner Life,* C. W. Leadbeater, 1922

## Physical Mediumship

*A Biography of the Brothers Davenport*, Thomas Low Nichols, 2007
*Alec Harris – The Full Story of His Remarkable Physical Mediumship,* Louise Harris, 2009
*'Best' of Both Worlds -: A Tribute to a Great Medium*, Rosalind Cattenach, 2016
*In Pursuit of Physical Mediumship*, Robin P. Foy, 2007
*Life After Death – Living Proof: A Lifetime's Experiences of Physical Phenomena and Materialisations Through the Mediumship of Minnie Harrison (Revised Edition),* Tom Harrison, 2008
*Manifesting Spirits: An Anthropological Study of Mediumship and the Paranormal*, Jack Hunter, 2020
*The complete D.D. Home Volume 1,* D.D. Home, 2007
*The Mediumship of Arnold Clare,* Harry Edwards, 2019

## Healing and Mediumship

*The Healing Intelligence,* Harry Edwards, 1965
*The Science of Spiritual Healing,* Harry Edwards, 1945
*Basic Principles of the Science of Mind*, Ernest Holmes, 1951

## Psychic Art and Artists

*How I Became a Psychic Artist,* Doris Strode, 2007
*Faces of the Living Dead,* Paul Miller, 2010

*Psychic Art – Two Books In One,* Saleire, 2014

*The Art of Psychic Reiki*: *Developing Your Intuitive and Empathic Abilities for Energy Healing,* Lisa Campion and Rhys Thomas, 2018

## Trance Mediumship

*A Glimpse of the Next State,* Vice Admiral W. Usborne Moore, 2009

*Resurrecting Leonora Piper: How Science Discovered the Afterlife,* Michael Tymn, 2013

*Trance Mediumship: Including Questions Answered by Her Spirit Guides,* Minister Judith Seaman, 2008

## Shamanism

*Astroshamanism: Journey into the Inner Universe Bk. 1,* Franco Santoro, 2003

*Astroshamanism: The Voyage Through the Zodiac Bk. 2,* Franco Santoro, 2003

*A Handbook on African Traditional Healing Approaches & Research,* Njoki Wane and Erica Neeganagwedgin, 2013

*A Handbook of Native American Herbs,* Alma R. Hutchens, 1992

*Ayahuasca visions*, Luis Eduardo Luna, 1999

*Called to Heal,* Susan Schuster Campbell, 2000

*Chosen by the Spirits: Following Your Shamanic Calling,* Sarangerel, 2001

*Healing Secrets of the Native Americans: Herbs, Remedies, and Practices That Restore the Body, Refresh the Mind, and Rebuild the Spirit,* Porter Shimer, 2004

*Healing the Exposed Being: The Ngoma Healing Tradition in South Africa,* Robert J. Thornton, 2007

*Honouring the Medicine: The Essential Guide to Native American Healing,* Ken Cohen, 2018

*Japanese Shamanism,* Percival Lowell, 2018

*Japanese Shamanism: Trance and possession,* Daniele Ricci, 2012

*Light of the Andes: In Search of Shamanic Wisdom in Peru,* J. E. Williams, 2012

*Maps to Ecstasy,* Gabriel Roth, 1999

*Masters of the Living Energy,* Joan Wilcox, 2004

*Native American Healing,* Howard Bad Hand, 2001

*Native American Healing Secrets: Mastering the Art of Native American Healing,* Emma Lee Walker, 2015

*On the wild edge of Sorrow,* Francis Weller, 2015

*Peruvian Shamanism*, Mathew Magee, 2002

*Shamanic Mysteries of Peru: The Heart Wisdom of the High Andes,* Linda Star Wolf, Jan. 2021

*Shaman: Invoking Power, Presence and Purpose at the Core of Who You Are,* Ya'Acov Darling Khan, 2020

*Shamans,* Ronald Hutton, 2007

*Shamanism in Siberia: Russian Records of Indigenous Spirituality,* Andrei A. Znamenski, 2010

*Shanar: Dedication Ritual of a Buryat Shaman in Siberia,* Sayan Zhambalov, Virlana Tkacz, and Wanda Phipps, 2016

*Siberian Shamanism,* Maria Czaplicka, 1914

*Siberian Shamanism: The Shanar Ritual of the Buryats,* Virlana Tkacz, 2016

*Spirits of the Earth: A Guide to Native American Nature Symbols, Stories,* Bobby Lake-Thom, 1997

*Sorcery And Shamanism,* Donald Joralemon, 1999

*Tengu: The Shamanic and Esoteric Origins of the Japanese Martial Arts,* Roald Knutsen, 2011

*The Book of the Dead,* E.A. Wallis Budge, 2008

*The Shaman's Coat,* Anna Reid, 2002

*The way of the Shaman,* Michael Harner, 1992

*Working with Spirit: Experiencing Izangoma Healing in Contemporary South Africa,* Joanne Wreford, 2008

## Earth Healing

*Earth Healing: Healing the Earth to Heal Ourselves,* Mahdi Mason, 2017

*Healing Mother Earth,* Kim Michaels, 2011

*Healing This Wounded Earth: With Compassion, Spirit and the Power of Hope*, Eleanor Stoneham, 2011

*The Healing Energies of Earth,* Liz Simpson, 2000

*The Healing of Gaia: How Children Saved the Earth,* M. C. Nelson, 2015

*Tom Brown's Guide to Healing the Earth,* Randy Walker and Tom Brown Jr., 2019

*Working With Earth Energies: How to Tap Into the Healing Powers of the Natural World,* David Furlong, 2017

*Women Healing Earth: Third World Women on Ecology, Feminism, and Religion,* Rosemary Radford Ruether, 2012

## Herbalism

*Herbal Healing for Women,* Rosemary Gladstar, 1993

*The Complete Illustrated Holistic Herbal: A Safe and Practical Guide to Making and Using Herbal Remedies,* David Hoffmann, 1996

*The Herbal Apothecary: 100 Medicinal Herbs and How to Use Them,* JJ Pursell, 2016
*The Herbal Handbook: A User's Guide to Medical Herbalism,* David Hoffmann, 1999
*The Herbal Medicine Maker's Handbook,* James Green, 2000

## Paranormal Investigations and Ghost Hunting

*A Brief Guide to Ghost Hunting,* Dr. Leo Ruickbie, 2013
*Ghost hunt Log, Selena Wright, 2015*
*Hunting Ghosts, A Paranormal Investigator Guide, Russel Vogels, 2014*
**Introduction to Parapsychology,** Eileen Garrett, 2011
*LLIFS Guide to EVP,* Sarah Chumacero, 2020
*Paranormal Investigators Need To Know Volume 1: What the eyes see and the ears hear the mind believes,* Sarah Chumacero - 2019
*Parapsychology,* Rhine and Pratt, 1957
*The A – Z British Ghosts,* Peter Underwood, 1993
*The Encyclopaedia of Ghosts and Spirits,* Rosemary Ellen Guiley, 2007

## Further Contacts and Organisations

The **Parapsychology Foundation** was founded by Eileen Garrett in 1951, who served as its President until her death in 1970. Following her death, her daughter Eileen Coly (1916-2013) became President. Lisette Coly, granddaughter of Eileen Garrett, served as Executive Director from 1978 and is now President of the Parapsychology Foundation.

**The Incorporated Society for Psychical Research**

1 Vernon Mews
London, W14 0RL

020 7937 8984 (UK)

secretary@spr.ac.uk

**www.spr.ac.uk**


'The Society for Psychical Research was set up in London in 1882, the first scientific organisation ever to examine claims of psychic and paranormal phenomena. We hold no corporate view about their existence or meaning; rather, our purpose is to gather information and foster understanding through research and education.'


**Arthur Findlay College**

01279 813636 (UK)

bookings@arthurfindlaycollege.org

**www.arthurfindlaycollege.org**

Arthur Findlay College, Stansted Hall, was gifted to the Spiritualists' National Union by J. Arthur Findlay, MBE, JP, a former Honorary President of the Union, and in accordance with his wishes is administered by the Union as a College for the advancement of Psychic Science.

**Theosophical Society England**

Headquarters:

50 Gloucester Place
London
W1U 8EA

020 7563 9817 (+44 20 7563 9817 – outside UK)

office@theosoc.org.uk

www.theosophicalsociety.org.uk

The Theosophical Society is a worldwide community whose primary object is the Universal Brotherhood of Humanity without distinction, based on the realisation that life and all its diverse forms, human and non-human, is indivisibly One.

Founded in 1875, the Society draws together those of goodwill whatever their religious affiliation (if any), social status, gender or ethnicity. The Society promotes such understanding through the study and practical application of the Ageless Wisdom of Theosophy.

## Ghost Club

c/o Flat 48, Woodside House

Woodside

London

SW19 7QN

UK

gensec@ghostclub.org.uk

**www.ghostclub.org.uk**

The Ghost Club is the oldest organisation in the world associated with psychical research. It was founded in 1862 but has its roots in Cambridge University where, in 1855, fellows at Trinity College began to discuss ghosts and psychic phenomena.

## The Sir Arthur Conan Doyle Centre

25 Palmerston Place
Edinburgh
EH12 5AP

0131 625 0700

info@arthurconandoylecentre.com

**www.arthurconandoylecentre.com**

The Sir Arthur Conan Doyle Centre first opened on 23rd of October 2011. We are a non-profit charity with a mission to make spirituality accessible to everyone. We achieve this by providing a space for the community to nurture their physical, mental and spiritual well-being

**Institute of Noetic Sciences**

101 San Antonio Rd.
Petaluma, CA 94952 USA
1(707)775 -3500
info@noetic.org

**www.noetic.org**

At the Institute of Noetic Sciences (IONS), we are inspired by the power of science to explain phenomena not previously understood, harnessing the best of the rational mind to make advances that further our knowledge and enhance our human experience.
The mission of the Institute of Noetic Sciences is to reveal the interconnected nature of reality through scientific exploration and personal discovery.

## **Acknowledgements**

I would like to thank all those who contributed to writing this book, knowingly or unknowingly.
Without you this would not have been possible.

First of all I would like to thank my family, especially Mum and Dad, for allowing me to explore my truth. My partner for his guidance and endless support, also our beloved dog Shady who always asked me out for a walk when everything got too much.

A special thanks to Susanne, Carrie, Anita Ratschiner and David – those people who always believed I had potential.

The teachers and fellow friends of the Arthur Findlay College fellow friends and teachers of the Arthur Findlay College (Bill Thomson, Ashley Wright, Kitty Wood, Jackie Wright, Andy Byng, Sandie Baker, Stella and Steven Upton, Paul Jacobs, Biaggio Tropeano, Tony Stockwell, Tanya Smith, John Johnson, Alan Stuttle, Judith Seamann, Angie Morris and others) who allowed me to learn so much about my personal gift and shared their knowledge and teachings with me. Furthermore, the teachers, mentors and friends I met along my personal spiritual path who allowed me to walk the path with them for a while.

The students and clients I had over the years who allowed me to explore new terrain and always asked the right questions.
All the guides and helpers, seen and unseen, who contributed to this important piece of work.

My astroshamanic Teacher, Franco Santoro, who assisted me in finally coming into my own, and who knows more than anyone else I ever met. May my work serve in accordance with the plan of Salvation and my Intent be connected with the function.

My editor, Rachel, for all her amazing input and putting my words into the right place. My web and cover designer, Ema, who always amazes me with her creative art.

Thank you to all those I have not mentioned but you know who you are.

Thank you universe
– for moving me through this



**Special Thanks To**

**RBR Paranormal Investigations**
For their endless support during our experiments, our work together with the Spirit Cabinet and Investigations as well as providing information about Parapsychology and Paranormal matters for this book.
Check out their Facebook page for Paranormal Investigations and lots of information and articles around the paranormal.
https://www.facebook.com/RBR-Paranormal-Investigations-148533965773920

**Sharon Shaw**
Holistic Alchemist, for her channelled picture
https://thegoldenspiral.co.uk

**Deanna Thomas**
Spiritual Therapies & Readings, for providing the Aura-graph pictures
Deanna is a spiritual & holistic therapist and energy worker based in the north-east of the UK.
https://www.facebook.com/deannathomastherapies

**Julie Events Artist**
For her Spirit Guide Paintings
Julie does individual Spirit Guide paintings and also gives you messages with it in your Reading.
https://www.facebook.com/ArtisticHolistic

**Claudia Hollenweger**
For her Aura-graph Paintings
Claudia speaks English and German and can do your personal Aura-graph and Reading via a distance if you email your request directly.
**info@praxismedialitaet.ch**
**www.praxismedialitaet.ch**


**Yogesh Kumar**
At Das Parfum, for giving me permission to share his story.
**www.dasparfum.com**
**Facebook:** Das Parfum
**Instagram:** dasparfum.yogesh
**Photo-credit:** www.diefotografin.at

**Resources/References:**

**Quote:** Aristotle – What is a friend - https://www.goodreads.com/quotes/18077-what-is-a-friend-a-single-soul-dwelling-in-two
**Quote:** Ernest Holmes, *Science of Mind* page: Intro xiii
**Quote:** Mary Sarton, https://www.brainyquote.com/quotes/may_sarton_156017
**Quote:** Albert Einstein, https://quoteinvestigator.com/2013/09/18/intuitive-mind/
**Quote:** Antoine de Saint-Exupery, https://www.brainyquote.com/quotes/antoine_de_saintexupery_101532

**Menstrual Cycle Awareness:** Alexandra Pope and Sjanie Hugo Wurlitzer – *Wild Power: Discover the magic of Your menstrual cycle and Awaken the Feminine Path to Power*, 2017, Publisher: Hay House, UK; Illustrated edition (4 April 2017)

**Mediumship:** Rosemary Ellen Guiley, *Encyclopaedia of Ghosts and Spirits*, pages 245/246 in 2001, Publisher: Facts On File Inc; 2nd edition (31 May 2001)

**Eileen Garrett Seance**, published in blog post at https://www.americanhauntingsink.com/garrett by American Hauntings Ink, 228 South Mauvaisterre Street, Jacksonsville, IL, 62650, United States (2020),

**Telepathy:** Eileen Garrett, *Adventures into the Supernormal*, p.133, 1949, Garrett Publications
(1 Jan. 1949)

**Rhine Zenner Cards Experiment:** Joseph Banks Rhine, 1934, *Extrasensory Perception*, Dukes University North Carolina

**Eileen Garrett on Rhines ESP:** *Adventures into the Supernormal*, pages 116/117, 1949, Garrett Publications (1 Jan. 1949)

**Edgar Cayce** – www.edgarcayce.org

**Apparitions:** Rosemary Ellen Guiley, *Encyclopaedia of Ghosts and Spirits*, page 245/246 in 2001, Publisher: Facts On File Inc; 2nd edition (31 May 2001)

**Azrael the Angel of Death** – Wikipedia 2020

**Remote Viewing:**

*Remote Viewing; What is it, who uses it and How to do it*, Tim Rifat, Publisher Vision Paperbacks 11 Oct. 2001

Stargate Project – Wikipedia 2020

CIA & Mars exploration – https://exopolitics.org/cia-used-remote-viewing-to-learn-about-mars-pyramids-inhabitants/

**Lady Townsend** – Wikipedia 2020

**Story of the Fox Sisters**
A Report of the Mysterious Noises - https://www.snu.org.uk/shop/a-report-of-the-mysterious-noises 1848,
Hydesville in History – M.E. Cadwallader
https://www.snu.org.uk/shop/hydesville-in-history-me-cadwallader (2020)

**Witch Trials** – http://www.spiritualist.tv/news/mar08/helen-duncan.html

**Salem Witch Trials** – https://www.smithsonianmag.com/history/a-brief-history-of-the-salem-witch-trials-175162489/

**The Spirituals' National Union** – https://www.snu.org.uk/about-us

**Table Tipping** – Wikipedia 2020

**Ouija Board** – - Source page 377, *The Encyclopaedia of Ghosts and Spirits* by Rosemary Ellen Guiley, Checkmark books, 2000

**Seances** – Wikipedia 2020

**Levitation**
Levitation of Monks – https://english.pravda.ru/society/9197-levitation/
Buddhist Monks Superpowers - https://universe-inside-you.com/buddhist-monks/
Levitation with Sound – https://www.bibliotecapleyades.net/ciencia/antigravityworldgrid/ciencia_antigravityworldgrid08.htm

**Pendulum** – https://pendulumpsychics.com/how-to-communicate-with-spirits-thru-a-pendulum/

**Ancient Rome and Mysticism**
https://mariamilani.com/ancient_rome/mysticism_signs_ancient_rome.htm
& Wikipedia 2020

**Greece**
Wikipedia 2020
Rise and Fall of Oracle of Delphi - https://www.pbs.org/empires/thegreeks/background/7_p1.html
Greek Sleeping Temples – Wikipedia 2020

**Quote:** Fernando Pesoa, https://www.goodreads.com/quotes/291646-my-soul-is-a-hidden-orchestra-i-know-not-what

**Clairaudience:** Eileen Garrett, Adventures into the Supernormal, p.131

**Healer Edgar Cayce** – www.edgarcayce.org/edgar-cayce/his-life/

**Quote:** Albert Einstein – https://www.goodreads.com/quotes/72237-i-believe-in-intuitions-and-inspirations-i-sometimes-feel-that-i

**Quote:** Friedrich Nietzsche – https://www.goodreads.com/quotes/9213-you-have-your-way-i-have-my-way-as-for

**Quote:** John Keats – https://www.goodreads.com/quotes/1120567-touch-has-a-memory-o-say-love-say-what-can

**Illustrations:**

a) Photograph of Stansted Hall from 1871 taken by Mr. and Mrs Wright of Stansted – published in Magazine on History of Essex

b) Picture of the Auras in emotional states of expression, licensed by adobe stock Nov. 2020

c) Woman sun heart space – licensed from adobe stock Nov. 2020

d) Woman meditating, licensed Fotolia in 2010

e) Woman light Solar plexus, licensed from adobe stock Nov. 2020

f) Recent Psychic Evidence is a letter written by Arthur Conan Doyle published in The New York Times on 2 September 1923. *Recent Psychic Evidence,* The New York Times (2 September 1923, section 7 p.10)

g) Young Edgar Cayce – Wikipedia 2020

h) Seance Flyer Eileen Garrett

i) Herbert Carmichael Irwin, 1929 Wikipedia 2020

j) Airship R101 in 1929, Wikipedia 2020

k) Entering into Dream State, licensed with Adobe Stock Nov. 2020

l) Lord Combe re: http://anomalyinfo.com/Stories/1891-december-5-lord-combermere-returns

m) Ghost apparition after fatal accident, 1998 taken by Sharon Boo, Fire brigade Volunteer Photographer

n) Zenner Cards, Wikipedia 2020

o) Eileen Garrett – contributed by Lisette Coley 2020

p) Apparition of Lady Townsend (1936), https://www.paranormal-encyclopedia.com/a/apparition/photos/images/brown-lady_02.jpg (2020)

q) Fox sisters, Wikipedia 2020

r) Fox Sisters Home, public domain 2020

s) Frederic W.H. Myers – Wikipedia 2020

t) Helen Duncan, en.wikipedia.org 2020

u) Old pic of table tipping, Wikipedia 2020

v) Modern Ouija Board by RBR Paranormal Investigations, 2020

w) Douglas D. Hume, Wikipedia 2020

x) Alec Harris Book, Amazon 2020

y) The Brothers Davenport, en. Wikipedia.org & their cabinet, weirdhistorian.com

1a) Ross Richards, cabinet, 2019

1b) Pendulum, Pixabay 2020

1c) Female Shaman, Vladimir Jochelson, Public domain, via Wikimedia Commons 2020

1d) Roman Empire Superstitions, http://factsanddetails.com/archives/003/201812/5c01ae76838d1.jpg, 2020

1e) Greek Oracle of Delphi, Tholos, Wikipedia 2020

1f) Prayer Hands, licensed by Adobe Stock 2020

1g) Ernest Holmes, 2020 http://www.newthoughtlibrary.com/holmesErnest/ErnestHolmes.jpg

1h) Music Waves, licensed by Fotolia 2010

1i) Channelled picture by Sharon Shaw

1j) Sleeping Temple, Asclepion, Wikipedia 2020

1k) Asclepios giving healing whilst people sleeping in temple, Wikipedia 2020

1l) Smudging tools (palo santo & sage) licensed adobe stock 2020

1m) Loch Ness Monster, public domain 2020

1n) Predict the Future, licensed by Adobe Stock 2020

1o) Soulpictures by Swiss Artist Claudia Hollenweger, 2020

1p) Pictures by UK Psychic Artist Julie Eventsartist, 2020

1q) Photos taken by Deanne Thomas, Holistic Therapist and Auraphotographer, 2020

1r) Cemetery, publicdomainpictures.net, 2020

1s) Leonora Piper, Wikipedia 2020

1t) Painting by Spiritualist Medium & Artist Elke Schneider, 2020

1u) John Campbell Sloan with his wife in 1946 – (Spirit Voice Phenomenon)

1v) Self-healing, an important Reiki practice, licensed adobe stock 2020

1w) Chakra in human body, public domain 2019

1x) Shamanic Drumming, licensed Adobe Stock 2020

1y) Crystals, licensed Adobe stock 2020

1z) Colour spiral, licensed Adobe stock 2020

Printed in Great Britain
by Amazon